Faith Exploration Series

Priesthood: For Others' Sake

By Alan D. Tyree

Paul M. Edwards
Series Editor

Priesthood: For Others' Sake

by
Alan D. Tyree

Faith Exploration Series

Paul M. Edwards
Series Editor

Herald Publishing House
Independence, Missouri

Copyright © 1996
Herald Publishing House
Independence, Missouri

Library of Congress Cataloging-in-Publication Data
Tyree, Alan D.
  Priesthood: for others' sake / by Alan D. Tyree.
    p. cm.—(Faith exploration series)
  Includes bibliographical references.
  ISBN 0-8309-0721-1
  1. Reorganized Church of Jesus Christ of Latter Day Saints—
Doctrines. 2. Priesthood (RLDS Church). I. Title. II. Series.
BX8675.T96 1996
262'.149333—DC20   95-44711
                                                              CIP

99 98 97 96   1 2 3 4

Contents

Foreword		7
I.	From Revelation to Priestly Society	9
II.	Two Theologies of Priesthood	17
III.	The Unfolding Panorama of Priesthood	31
IV.	Two Models for Priestly Ministry	41
	Ordinations and Offices	45
	Women Disciples	57
	Wolves among the Flock	65
V.	Priesthood in the Reorganization	69
VI.	Priesthood Today	73
	Differentiation in Priesthood	80
	Authority in Priesthood	84
VII.	Conclusion	97
Bibliography and Suggested Readings		103
Study Guide		105

Foreword

This is the first in a new series of monographs published by Herald House under the title "Faith Exploration Series." Series editor Paul Edwards, director of Temple School Center and dean of the Park College Graduate School of Religion, has enlisted the efforts of many of the leading theologians, scholars, and educators in the RLDS community to write these books. A study guide will accompany each, making them ideal for use in class settings for adults and senior-high-age youth.

The genesis for this project actually was more than twenty-five years ago with the publication of *Exploring the Faith: A Series of Studies in the Faith of the Church Prepared by a Committee on Basic Beliefs* (Herald House, 1970). That landmark effort, which represented the efforts of many church leaders and educators, was spearheaded by President F. Henry Edwards and Apostle Clifford A. Cole. The Foreword to that book, over the signature of the First Presidency, included the following:

> It is fully intended that the work of the committee in developing the concise statements and interpretative articles will provide members of the priesthood, laity of the church, and inquiring friends with the basis for intense personal and corporate study in the years to come. Such a work is never finished because each generation brings its own unique insights and experience to the task. Of necessity there is a continuity in the history of religious experience so that any generation cannot regard itself as standing alone without meaningful relationship to the past and to the future.

In 1987 Herald House published a revised edition of *Exploring the Faith*. Like its predecessor, it sparked ongoing discussion and debate about the church's beliefs. Alan D. Tyree, at that time a member of the First Presidency, edited and updated the earlier work of the Basic Beliefs Committee. Coincidentally, Brother Tyree, now retired from forty-one years of World Church appointee ministry, has written the first in what we hope will be many interesting and challenging monographs.

Roger Yarrington

* * *

The Restoration was born amidst the promises of a deeply examined faith. For young Joseph, the divine call was strong but undefined. In his desire to understand, he found his mission. It was his willingness to investigate the borders of his own faith that eventually led to the formation of the Church of Christ. This same desire to expand beyond the limitations of a narrow faith and to develop a greater understanding and response to a growing awareness of our Creator has marked the Reorganized Church of Jesus Christ of Latter Day Saints from the beginning. Members have always placed great significance on the faith examination which accompanies a vital spiritual journey.

This series on Faith Exploration is a part of that eternal journey. Many of the primary questions of our beliefs and convictions are examined. The role of priesthood is fundamental. In this work, Alan D. Tyree, former counselor to President Wallace B. Smith, takes a serious look at the concept of priesthood within the Christian Church and focuses on this responsibility in the life of the RLDS Church.

Paul M. Edwards

From Revelation to Priestly Society

As Moses traveled through the barren desert lands, probably his thoughts were turning to respite from the heat, relief for his dusty and dehydrated body—and water, which would assuage most of his needs. He was not expecting to find God. Nor was he expecting to find God in a fire! The burden of the desert was enough to induce heat-laden eyes to search, naturally and without thought, for living vegetation—signs of an oasis and water—not for a fire. But here was a miraculous fire that could envelope a bush without consuming it, and that was reason enough to divert Moses from his journey and concern for his own needs, to see what magic was at work just off the trail. His curious mind, schooled in the science and superstitions of Egypt, was attracted to something most extraordinary happening on the fringe of his knowledge. God knew how to attract Moses' attention, and to hold it with an image that would forever remain in his memory and that of his people, and their descendants from generation to generation throughout the centuries.

From the earliest times, humanity has experienced an awareness of the Divine moving and acting in our world. Our Judeo-Christian heritage is filled with ancient stories of how God confronted our ancestors, bringing purpose and guidance to their lives. And in every instance, Deity has elicited a response of awe and an awareness of mystery. There has always been the feeling that God *surprised* us by self-disclosure or by some display of divine power. It was not as if some one of us consciously set about to create God, or through personal effort invented a means to discover God.

Jews and Christians alike testify that it was always the Divine who apprehended the human rather than the human apprehending the Divine. As the anonymous but worthy hymn writer has written,

> I sought the Lord, and afterward I knew
>   He moved my soul to seek him, seeking me;
> It was not I that found, O Savior true;
>   No; I was found of thee.
>
> Thou didst reach forth thy hand and mine enfold;
>   I walked and sank not on the storm-vexed sea;
> 'Twas not so much that I on thee took hold
>   As thou, dear Lord, on me.
>
> I find, I walk, I love, but oh, the whole
>   Of love is but my answer, Lord, to thee!
> For thou were long beforehand with my soul:
>   Always thou didst love me.[1]

Such divine self-disclosure revealed divine grace. Those who received this revelation knew they were somehow *favored* to have a new form of correspondence with God, a higher relationship than they had known. Whether it was generally recognized by their tribe, family, village, or culture—or whether no one else at all was aware of it—the individual *knew* that God had intervened in a way that was uncommon.

With the gift of the spiritual experience came another gift also: a sense of being chosen. Whether it was a person or a people sharing in a common experience, it was the same: they felt called out from the ordinary stream of their peers. This concept of vocation, of calling, was implied in the divine revelation.

A famous instance of this phenomenon, in both its individual and collective expression, is the exodus of the children of Israel from Egypt. God had spoken out of the burning bush, and Moses was forever held by the knowledge that God had chosen him for a particular task. When Moses began to act on the basis of that knowledge, he attracted followers among the Israelites in Egypt who were eager to participate in the liberating divine purpose. After they had all shared together in the plagues, the Passover, the Exodus, and the trials that followed in the wilderness, they had lived through a common revelatory experience of divine direction and calling. It was a collective experience, the happenings in the life of a people. Not only was Moses called out of the burning bush, all of Israel was also called, and they came to recognize the divine grace in a shared history of being led by God.

A body of chosen representatives—priesthood—is a natural result of God's and humanity's attempts to carry out the intentions of the revelatory experience. After Moses had brought the Israelite tribes out of Egypt into the wilderness, an entire system of social organization had to be developed, otherwise their fate could have been worse than to have remained in Egypt. If they were truly to become a free people, much work was needed to bring about their freedom.

In some ways, it is analogous to the situation in Haiti following the recent coup against the government. For almost two centuries, Haitians have been living under the rule of dictatorial leaders. Democracy and the liberties enjoyed by free nations are not understood by either the leaders or the masses in that country. Such a situation cannot be turned around in a few weeks or years—perhaps not even in a generation or two. Similarly, the leaders among the newborn Israelite nation required more than forty years in the wilderness to begin the socialization process needed to transform the people.

The government was theocratic: divine leadership through the divinely appointed leaders. It brought a social ethic to the people and held up moral demands for regulating everyday behavior. Priesthood played an important role. It came as a natural result of the revelation at the burning bush and the ongoing revelation of a history shared with God and a day-to-day theocratic leadership.

It was only a matter of time before that priestly leadership would become institutionalized. Numerical growth, the increasing complexity of their society, and demanding international and interracial matters required their attention and influenced their decisions. They were themselves a part of the changing scene, acting and acted upon. They were in a position to influence changes in Israelite society. Priesthood adjusted to changing circumstances and exerted its influence on the changes.

Further, priesthood developed as a means of dealing with all sorts of religious experiences operating among the children of Israel, with which they identified subjectively in varying degrees. Much of it was influenced by their pagan neighbors.

> And the children of Israel dwelt among the Canaanites, Hittites, and Amorites, and Perizzites, and Hivites, and Jebusites; and they took their daughters to be their wives, and gave their daughters to their sons, and served their gods.—Judges 3:5-6

It was no small task to attenuate this erosion of their identity and faith, much less prevent it.

William G. Dever, professor and archeologist specializing in Near Eastern studies, in his book *Recent Archeological Discoveries and Biblical Research*, published in 1990, said about this period:

> Yahweh, the god of Israel, was unattested outside the Bible until modern research and excavation placed this deity in the context of ancient Near Eastern history and religion through parallel textual discoveries, including the first actual occurrence of the name "Yahweh" in Hebrew inscriptions only a few years ago. But archaeology now confirms (as the Bible hints) that other deities, specifically Canaanite fertility gods, were revered in ancient Israel. Chief among them were the "Mother Goddess" Asherah...and the "Storm God" Ba'al, whom the Israelites apparently regarded as her consort.... Thus it is clear that in ancient Israel, until the Exile, Asherah and Ba'al were not shadowy numina, dead and discredited gods of old Canaan. Rather, the pair were potent rivals of Yahweh himself, and for the masses their cult, with its promise of integration with the very life-giving forces of Nature, remained an attractive alternative to the more austere religion and ethical demands of Yahwism.[2]

Such problems had to be dealt with in an organized way that authenticated only the truly divine experiences, and authorized those who would receive and promulgate those experiences. False and errant leaders, as well as beliefs and practices had to be regulated, and evaluated against the norms: a divinely called leadership, orthodox belief, and a revealed ethic. This led to practices that, to us today, in some instances seem cruel and unchristian.

For example, chapters nine and ten of Ezra illustrate the function of the priesthood in matters of ethics, religion, sociology, and government. The priest Ezra had such respect and power over the people that, when they feared they had offended Yahweh and were publicly repentant for their offense, he could require Israelite men to reject their pagan wives and separate themselves from them and their children out of loyalty to Yahweh. It is interesting that the Bible records "the people wept very sore" (10:1)—not at the tearing apart of families, but in contrition over their offense against Yahweh.

In a theocratic state, where religion is in charge of government and the name of God is invoked as the ultimate authority for everything that happens, we would expect the major functions of society to be organized and regulated by faith. It is not without reason that the newspapers in Israel today publish the precise times for the rising and the setting of the sun with several minutes to spare, rather than observing the strict meteorological times, as a public service to avoid an accidental infringement of sabbath requirements. The stronger the influence of religion on society, the more obvious is its presence by its functions, and the more power its religious leaders can exercise. If the priesthood are also the political leaders, then their power is virtually absolute.

It is relatively simple for us to observe the pragmatic functions of priesthood in bringing government to a society, and in authorizing and authenticating its leaders and beliefs. That is what happened in ancient Israel, when the nation functioned as a theocracy with rule by God and God's chosen priesthood. But if we can see that picture rather clearly, can we use it to define priesthood? By describing priesthood's functions, which have varied so much through the ages under the many forms of government exercising authority over God's people, do we create a contemporary definition of priesthood? The range of priestly functions spans the gamut from those practiced under theocratic nationalism to those permitted a suppressed minority in ghetto isolation. Is it a complete answer to define priesthood by saying that "priesthood is what priesthood does" if the deeds and duties of priesthood are always subject to change? For any approximation of an answer to these questions, we need to inquire after priesthood's origins, its source, its meaning, and its ultimate purpose.

Two Theologies of Priesthood

The History of the Reorganized Church of Jesus Christ of Latter Day Saints (I: 34–39) gives accounts by Joseph Smith Jr. and Oliver Cowdery of their spiritual experience with the angel, identified as John the Baptist. It is the occasion when priesthood authority was conferred on them—May 15, 1829. They wrote interesting and somewhat differing accounts of the experience. First, Joseph's account:

> We still continued the work of translation, when in the ensuing month...we on a certain day went into the woods to pray and inquire of the Lord respecting baptism for the remission of sins, as we found mentioned in the translation of the plates. While we were thus employed, praying, and calling upon the Lord, a messenger from heaven descended in a cloud of light, and having laid his hands upon us, he ordained us, saying unto us, "Upon you, my fellow servants, in the name of Messiah, I confer the priesthood of Aaron, which holds the keys of the ministering of angels, and of the gospel of repentance, and of baptism by immersion, for the remission of sins..." and he commanded us to go and be baptized, and gave us directions....
>
> The messenger who visited us on this occasion, and conferred this priesthood upon us, said that his name was John, the same that is called John the Baptist, in the New Testament,

and that he acted under the direction of Peter, James, and John, who held the keys of the priesthood of Melchisedec.[3]

Next, Oliver's account:

The Lord, who is rich in mercy, and ever willing to answer the consistent prayer of the humble, after we had called upon him in a fervent manner, aside from the abodes of men, condescended to manifest to us his will. On a sudden, as from the midst of eternity, the voice of the Redeemer spake peace to us, while the vail [sic] was parted and the angel of God came down clothed with glory, and delivered the anxiously looked for message, and the keys of the gospel of repentance! What joy! what wonder! what amazement!... our eyes beheld—our ears heard. As in the "blaze of day;" yes, more—above the glitter of the May sunbeam, which then shed its brilliancy over the face of nature! Then his voice, though mild, pierced to the center, and his words, "I am thy fellow-servant," dispelled every fear. We listened—we gazed—we admired! 'Twas the voice of the angel from glory... and we were rapt in the vision of the Almighty! Where was room for doubt? Nowhere: uncertainty had fled, doubt had sunk, no more to rise, while fiction and deception had fled forever!

But, dear brother, think, further think for a moment, what joy filled our hearts and with what surprise we must have bowed...when we received under his hand the holy priesthood, as he said, "Upon you my fellow-servants, in the name of Messiah, I confer this priesthood and this authority...".

I shall not attempt to paint to you the feelings of this heart, nor the majestic beauty and glory which surrounded us on this occasion; but you will believe me when I say, that earth, nor men, with the eloquence of time, cannot begin to clothe language in as interesting and sublime a manner as this holy personage. No; nor has this earth power to give the joy, to bestow the peace, or comprehend the wisdom which was contained in each sentence as they were delivered by the power of the Holy Spirit!... The assurance that we were in the presence of an angel; the certainty that we heard the voice of Jesus, and the truth unsullied as it flowed from a pure personage, dictated by the will of God, is to me, past description....[4]

There are two major ways by which priesthood is defined: (1) that priesthood is eternal, absolute and universal; and (2) that priesthood can only exist in human history. The first of these emphasizes the divine origins of priesthood at the expense of human involvement. Because priesthood as a concept is entirely related with the human experiences of God, in the minds of many believers it easily partakes of some of the same attributes as God possesses. If priesthood is conferred by angels, then it is not unreasonable to expect that angelic ministry and powers accompany the gift, as Joseph testified. If we believe that priesthood is created and given by a God who is eternal, absolute and universal, then some of us certainly will believe in a priesthood which is eternal, absolute, and universal. And if the priesthood system that is intermediary between God and humanity possesses some divine attributes, then the individual intermediary is also often thought, and perhaps expected, to possess some of God's own attributes.

In fact, members of the priesthood are *expected* by everybody to be holier than the average member of the church body. The unscrupulous televangelist is doubly condemned because he is supposed to be holier than the common Christian. These expectations exist because of the *way* in which God breaks into one's awareness, causing at the same time (1) an understanding of some sort about God's nature, and (2) an awareness of one's unique favor in having been chosen as an intermediary for this experience and for its future consequences.

Although, fortunately, it may not occur frequently, it is nevertheless true that the experiences we think have come from God, and the meanings we take from our experiences with God, may be mutually contradictory when compared. It has happened, at least once, that a conference of the Saints heard testimony from two brothers of the faith, each claiming he had received divine light through a spiritual experience concerning the calling of another brother to priesthood. But their convictions were diametrically opposed: God had told one that the brother was called to a certain office, and God had told the other that he was not.

On a larger scale, the question of the ordination of women brought forth many testimonies, both pro and con, all claiming divine approbation for their points of view. Revelation from God is, at least, filtered through a human mind before it is heard by others.

Leaving this narrow concept of calls to priesthood, in principle the broader question of all revelatory experience, no matter what the content, is similarly very subjectively focused. It makes little difference that an anthropologist may be able to document the influences, both physical and psychological, that may have had a part in creating the spiritual experience or illusion of an experience. The supreme fact is the person experiences as real whatever the person *thinks* he or she experiences.

If God is thought to be *acting* in our human world, then we humans will see ourselves as *reacting* to the divine initiative. When that action is felt personally, we feel personally favored and called by God. This sense of calling accompanies the revelation received from God: they both come out of the same spiritual experience.

Isaiah's experience of worship, vision, revelation, and calling is one such experience. Chapter 6 tells us he was in the temple worshiping when he saw a vision of the Lord. And in that moment of exalted worship, it was revealed to him just how sinful he and his people were in the sight of God. "Woe is me! for I am undone; because I am a man of unclean lips, and I dwell in the midst of a people of unclean lips." When he sensed the awfulness of their unrepentant state, he was moved to repentance and found the Lord willing to forgive. "Then flew one of the seraphim unto me, having a live coal in his hand...and he laid it upon my mouth, and said, Lo, this has touched thy lips; and thine iniquity is taken away, and thy sin purged." It is in this same revelatory experience that he hears his call to specific ministry. "Whom shall I send, and who will go for us?" And Isaiah responds, "Here am I; send me" (Isaiah 6:5–8).

The RLDS Church believes that the call to priesthood comes by the medium of revelatory experience—in the one calling the new ordinand and also to the one being called. Because of this belief, the holiness of the revelatory process may become associated with the new ordinand. Some of the qualities of holiness understood to exist in the prophecy also are thought to dwell in the prophet and the one designated by the prophet. It is very dangerous for priesthood members to believe their holiness exceeds that of others. Such a belief carries the potential for perverted use of priesthood for personal gain of some sort. But it is still quite true that many people so regard those who hold ministerial office.

Whether or not someone views an individual minister with such qualities of holiness, many people assume that God's attributes of eternity, priority, and universality also inhere in the "favoredness" of priesthood as an entity. This is a result of the belief that priesthood holds the keys of access to God. If God is eternal, has always existed, and is present everywhere and always, then the gift of the keys of access to God (priesthood) may also be imbued with those same divine qualities. Priesthood may, therefore, be thought by some to be preexistent, eternal, absolute, and universal because God is seen that way, and priesthood is seen as our closest tie to God.

Our first look at the testimonies of Oliver and Joseph certainly appears to suggest they understood priesthood to relate to God and humanity in that way. Priesthood dwelt in eternity with God before being granted to humans, and it was conferred by divine commandment through the intermediary of the angel John the Baptist, historically known as a prophet of God. If it can be given in 1829 to Joseph and Oliver, then God can give it at any time and to anyone God chooses. Priesthood, therefore, shares some of God's qualities of eternity and universality.

However, we should ask ourselves if we are warranted in holding such perceptions and in placing this interpretation on the experiences of Joseph and Oliver. Is priesthood, as such, eternal? That is, does it exist beyond the time and space limitations we humans experience in this earthly life? Does it somehow exist independently of people and their existence? If so, how? Is it like the Godhead, transcending our earthly limitations? Or is it only to be observed in its practical usages for the benefit of humanity as a God-ordained means of blessing and leading and communicating with God's creation? Does it, in fact, really have any use or purpose if it exists in a nonhuman situation?

Advocates of this definition of priesthood would profess a belief that priesthood's essence does exist in God, apart from its human expression. It is thought to have been granted by God from time to time, somewhat intermittently, to deserving and qualified persons, historically only men. Proponents of this point of view believe that priesthood has a life of its own, separate from the individuals who have been ordained to specific priesthood offices. It, therefore, can come and go, enter and depart, from the stream of human history.

Does such a concept of priesthood square with all else that we know about reality and God? Is priesthood different from all other human experiences and categories, dwelling in an ethereal realm that only occasionally catches up the human into a mystical relationship with the Divine? Or is priesthood a category of human experience, set apart from all others, perhaps, but nonetheless fully integrated into the totality of life? Is priesthood what priesthood does, functionally (nominalism)? Or is priesthood what priesthood is conceived to be (realism)?

There is another way of defining priesthood. Others take the opposite point of view and believe that priesthood, by its very nature, can only exist in human history, in the particular individuals who carry out its functions in the context of culture, in the midst of human life. Those who profess this belief do not necessarily deny some measure of transcendence and eternal qualities to priesthood but would suggest that it is rather more like our deceased priesthood ministers whose priesthood continues with them into eternal life. In this sense, the way that priesthood transcends our present limitations is more like the way our loved ones live on spiritually after death, than the way the Godhead transcends the human dimensions of life.

Joseph Smith Jr. left some scriptural indications that are subject to various interpretations. Some may read these passages and find support for their belief in a universal, transcendent, eternal priesthood. These scriptures may be interpreted to suggest that we are warranted in holding a belief in a priesthood that exists as universal essence, eternal and absolute, and therefore existing independently of human manifestations of priesthood. Consider Hebrews 7:3 in the Inspired Version:

> ...which order [of priesthood] was without father, without mother, without descent, having neither beginning of days, nor end of life. And all those who are ordained unto this priesthood....[abide] a priest continually.

Doctrine and Covenants 83:2g and 3a adds:

> ...which priesthood continueth in the church of God in all generations, and is without beginning of days or end of years...which priesthood also continueth and abideth forever...

But those persuaded of the opposing view would suggest that the "order of priesthood" exists without father, mother, and descendant, and without beginning or ending, due to the fact that it does not at all exist independent of the particular priests who collectively compose priesthood. The priests obviously do have a father and a mother and maybe descendants and do have a beginning and an ending. But the sum of them does equal more than an adding of finite individuals together with other finite individuals, for they may succeed one another, providing priesthood with a quality of transcendence.

Priesthood may have patterns of succession that exceed finitude, permitting a continuity of succession. If a father is succeeded by his son, then the father's priesthood continues in the son. If one generation of priests is followed by another, then the first generation's priesthood finds continuity in the second generation. Thus priesthood may "continue and abide forever" as long as humans exist to carry the lineage.

Furthermore, believing in eternal life for humans also establishes a continuation of priesthood into eternity by virtue of the priests who carry their priesthood with them into eternal life. If the qualities of personhood and personality continue after death in the eternal life of the departed, then among those qualities must be the very ones that permit ministry to be given in the name of the Lord. Therefore the "priestly-ness" (or priesthood) of the person accompanies the priest who has died into the realms of eternal life, and becomes eternal with the person. Human eternal life imparts eternal qualities to priesthood itself through the priests who are bearers both of eternal life and priesthood.

This definition of priesthood further suggests that if priesthood is "eternal," then it is so by virtue of its *particularity*, not its universality. It is particular priests who hold priesthood, and they as individuals embody priesthood, giving it its particularity. But they are also destined, if faithful, for eternal life with God, and their embodiment of priesthood is taken with them into eternal life. Such a condition gives priesthood its quality of eternity.

Care should be taken as to what is meant by priesthood becoming eternal through individual priesthood members. It has long been believed by the Restoration churches that the passages cited above from Doctrine and Covenants 83:2–3 and Hebrews 7:3 IV are inspired writing, and, therefore, contain some serious elements of revelation and truth from God. The LDS (Mormon) and RLDS Churches have taken quite different views of how this eternal quality functions in their theological projections of life after death. For the Mormon understanding, a serious student should consult writings by Mormon authors. Their approach is, in general, an integration of priesthood and its keys of authority into a complete plan of salvation for all humankind, extending progressively into worlds beyond this universe.

The RLDS position, on the other hand, has been more a projection of priesthood's ministerial nature, a servanthood that continues in life after death. This view is perhaps modeled after New Testament understandings of the ministry of Jesus following his crucifixion.

> For Christ also once suffered for sins, the just for the unjust, being put to death in the flesh, but quickened by the Spirit, that he might bring us to God. For which cause also, he went and preached unto the spirits in prison; some of whom were disobedient in the days of Noah... Because of this, is the gospel preached to them who are dead, that they might be judged according to men in the flesh, but live in the spirit according to the will of God.—I Peter 3:18–20, 4:6

This and other similar passages from the scriptures have been interpreted by RLDS members to suggest that ministry is needed in life after death and that priesthood continues to serve that need.

Incidents from church history appear to support the concept that individual priesthood members may continue their ministry, not only in the spirit world, but also in the form of angelic ministry here on earth. Joseph Smith Jr. and Oliver Cowdery testified that it was the angel John the Baptist who conferred on them the authority to ordain each other to the Aaronic priesthood. They imply that John's priesthood continued with him, permitting him to grant the same authority to themselves. The quality of priesthood inhering in the individual continued with the person into life after death—therefore giving to priesthood its eternal quality.

Joseph Smith also brought to the church the scripture that says that "the elements are eternal" (Doctrine and Covenants 90:5). Thomas Aquinas said that if universals exist in things as their essence, then things are made individual by their matter. That is, if the universal idea of priesthood exists in individual members of priesthood as the essence of priesthood in them, then the priesthood members are made particular manifestations of universal priesthood by virtue of their material nature. However, Joseph Smith Jr.'s statement that "the elements are eternal" would suggest the contrary.

Joseph's statement concords well with the scientific principle of conservation of matter and energy. If the subatomic particles, the "stuff" out of which all that exists is made, are eternal, and human life is eternal, then it follows that priesthood is not held captive in its particularity to this earthly existence: it, too, may be eternal. It is because humans with their earthly qualities are intended for eternity that priesthood's particularity in them becomes universal and eternal. Thus priesthood's particularity is cause for its universality and eternal qualities. Due to the individual priest participating in human life and, therefore, partaking of physical and material existence, the elements of matter, being eternal, foresee an eternal quality to the individual's priesthood.

Inasmuch as priesthood is described by Joseph Smith Jr. in several scriptures as being "without father or mother," it may be presumed that he is suggesting that priesthood is universal, and that individuals may share temporarily in the essence of the universal as they are divinely called and ordained. According to this presumption, they are born of father and mother, but priesthood is not, and continues without earthly parents. Yet when taken in the context of Joseph Smith's other scriptural statements, such as "the elements are eternal," we are exposed to a different facet of his thinking. If priesthood is "without father or mother, beginning or ending," does it necessarily follow that it is *in itself* preexistent, eternal, and universal? It might rather be that priesthood is without beginning or ending because it always and only exists in humans. If its essence can only be found in the particular, then it is as eternal as the particular is. Joseph Smith Jr. said that not only does the human spirit continue after death, but that the elements composing the material universe (hence the human embodiment) are also eternal. Thus if humans are eternal, and if priesthood is found only in humans, then it may be that priesthood continues because of its expression in individual humans.

Particularity and nominalism (the practical, useful functioning of priesthood) are as logical an interpretation for Joseph Smith's scriptural expressions as may be universalism and realism (priesthood as an eternal entity in concept).

There are some compelling reasons why it is difficult for us to accept the idea of priesthood existing absolutely or universally, independent from any particular expression. First, the concept of universals and absolutes appears to have had its origin in Greek thought, not in Judeo-Christian developments. This requires us to look to the possibility of a cultural source rather than a revealed source for even the concept of the universal/absolute itself.

Second, history shows that priesthood's changes over the ages have been related pragmatically to circumstances of culture and exigency. This again suggests nominalism rather than realism, particularity rather than universalism. Later chapters will explore this in some detail, noting the impact of cultural considerations on the evolution of priesthood from Old Testament and New Testament times and from the more recent history of the Restoration movement.

Third, take into consideration that the authoritarian churches are dependent on the universal view for support to much of their theology. Churches such as the Catholic, Orthodox, and Mormon espouse a polity grounded in theism, belief in an immanent and personal God who governs the church through a priesthood hierarchy. Theological questions such as the fall, sin, salvation, moral law, and the church are answered: all are universally condemned under the first fall; all are sinners; all are saved through

Christ's atonement; all are subject to a universal moral law; Christ established one universal church—and each authoritarian church believes itself to be that one church.

Although it may not be necessarily so, in practice it appears that most (or perhaps all) such theocratic churches combine government by the clergy with a universalistic or realistic view of priesthood. It becomes questionable, therefore, whether a church that identifies itself as a "theocratic democracy," as does the RLDS Church, can accept a universalistic position and remain a balanced theocratic democracy. Realism and universalism may bring in their train a polity that is more theistic (that is, God and priesthood directed) and less democratic (directed by the people) than our church perceives itself to be.

The weight of the evidence requires us to look at priesthood as being particular, that is, rooted in human history, evolving in human culture, serving divine and universal purposes (as best these may be understood) but within a context of human society. For Latter Day Saints, the "cause of Zion" is the bringing together of the divine intent into the affairs of the human social order for the redemption of society, or the building up of the kingdom of God on earth. For our faith and our beliefs about priesthood and Zion to be consistent, a nominalistic view of priesthood as existing in the particular individuals who are called to be priests may be indicated.

The Unfolding Panorama of Priesthood

In ancient times, priesthood was not necessary for the performance of sacrificial functions. Although sacrifice was an important form of worship, anyone could offer burnt offerings. Not only is this the viewpoint of scholars of Old Testament and Hebrew history, it also appears that Joseph Smith Jr.'s scriptural emendations supports this understanding. In Genesis 4:4–10 IV, Adam's first sacrificial offerings appear to have been made early in his life experience, before the development of priesthood.

> And Adam called upon the name of the Lord, and Eve also, his wife; and they heard the voice of the Lord, from the way towards the garden of Eden, speaking unto them.... And he gave unto them commandments, that they...should offer the firstling of their flocks for an offering unto the Lord. And Adam was obedient unto the commandments of the Lord.

Further support for this point of view appears in the insight Joseph Smith brought in Doctrine and Covenants 104:18–28, indicating that priesthood was instituted sometime during Adam's extraordinarily long lifetime, spanning more than nine centuries. "The order of this priesthood...was instituted in the days of Adam, and came down by lineage in the following manner: From Adam to Seth, who was ordained by Adam at the age of sixty-nine years...". However, there appears no suggestion either in Genesis or Doctrine and Covenants that priesthood was necessary for the offering of sacrifice during the earliest times.

Originally, there was no requirement that Levites or priests or a special family or tribe should provide for this function. These requirements came later, after the exodus of Israel from Egypt. When priesthood appeared as a functioning authority, it came into the context of a society that was already patriarchal. Consequently, priesthood originally was conferred only on males. The earliest forms of Israelite priesthood had to do more with caring for and guarding the sanctuary and its appurtenances after which were developed means for serving the worship of the people.

Priesthood also functioned to consult the prophetic oracle. The Urim and Thummim, along with the ephod to which the breastplate was attached, were used as a means of consulting the oracle for answers that would establish right from wrong, yes from no, true from false, and, in the judicial function, guilty from not guilty. It was for this reason that the breastplate was called a "breastplate of judgment" (Exodus 28:15, 29). Thus criminal cases were appealed to the priest for judgment as being "brought before God," inasmuch as the priest could consult the oracle, the Urim and Thummim.

An instance of the use of Urim and Thummim is described in I Samuel 23:8–12:

> And Saul called all the people together to war, to go down to Keilah, to besiege David and his men. And David knew that Saul secretly practiced mischief against him; and he said to Abiathar the priest, Bring hither the ephod [which contained the Urim and Thummim]. Then said David, O Lord God of Israel, thy servant hath certainly heard that Saul seeketh to come to Keilah, to destroy the city for my sake. Will the men of Keilah deliver me up into his hand? will Saul come down, as thy servant hath heard?... And the Lord said, He will come down. Then said David, Will the men of Keilah deliver me and my men into the hand of Saul? And the Lord said, They will deliver thee up.

In such cases, the function of the priest was to formally consult the Urim and Thummim in a worshipful attitude, seeking the mind of God. The answer was not verbal, but rather in the form of a casting of lots, for it could be a "yes" or "no" answer, as in this instance. It was understood by David that it was God who spoke when the priest obtained an answer by using the Urim and Thummim, and David acted accordingly.

The Urim and Thummim were carried in the breastplate which was made of linen, fine stones, and gold lacings as described in Exodus 28:15–28. The breastplate was made integral with the ephod, which was also of "fine twined linen" (vss. 6, 15). "And they shall bind the breastplate by the rings thereof unto the rings of the ephod with a lace of blue...that the breastplate be not loosed from the ephod" (vs. 28). "And thou shalt put in the breastplate of judgment the Urim and the Thummim; and they shall be upon Aaron's heart, when he goeth in before the Lord..." (vs. 30). Thus when David asked the priest Abiathar to bring the ephod, he was in fact asking for everything attached to it: breastplate and

Urim and Thummim. It was the prophetic function he sought and heeded.

When did these early priesthood functions begin? We should note, first of all, that the scriptures do not suggest a fully developed priesthood ministry, replete with differentiated functions and offices, such as later eras and modern times possess. The Inspired Version of the Bible, as modified by Joseph Smith and Sidney Rigdon, suggests an antiquity to the priesthood that is not verified elsewhere. "Now this same priesthood which was in the beginning, shall be in the end of the world also" (Genesis 6:7 IV).

It is not clear in the book of Genesis, Inspired Version, what the total ministry of priesthood encompassed. From the story of Adam's observance of the commandment (Genesis 4:5) to offer sacrifice to God, it is apparent in the Inspired Version that it was incumbent on everyone to worship God in this manner, and that ordination to priesthood was not required in order to serve this function. Section 104:19a of the Doctrine and Covenants indicates a rather late ordination for Adam's son, Seth, at age sixty-nine, although Genesis 6:4 implies that Seth offered sacrifices much earlier. It can be inferred from verse 7 that Adam held some priesthood responsibility, but it is unclear what that entailed, or when and by whom ordination occurred. It may be that what is implied is the continuation of the propagation of the gospel described in Genesis 5:44–45:

> And thus the gospel began to be preached from the beginning, being declared by holy angels, sent forth from the presence of God; and by his own voice; and by the gift of the Holy Ghost. And thus all things were confirmed unto Adam by

an holy ordinance; and the gospel preached; and a decree sent forth that it should be in the world until the end thereof....

What other priesthood functions were expected and practiced is not known from this source.

Section 104:18–19 of the Doctrine and Covenants, while suggesting that whatever priesthood Adam was given was also passed on to his descendants, does not reveal, within the account, how priesthood functioned. Conjecture is of little value to us in attempting to reconstruct what possibly may have been the purposes of priesthood at such an early time, because of cultural and environmental circumstances, which are beyond one's ability to imagine or reconstruct. But sacrificial offerings did not require priesthood. It was a later elaboration of this function that assigned it to the Levites.

Other sources also do not provide any historical corroboration of priesthood being inherited through lineage from as early a time as Adam's time forward. Instead, other records, especially other books of the Bible, record that priesthood began to be inherited and passed from generation to generation during the same early period when a chief function was to consult the oracle. That period is the time of Moses' leadership, after the Exodus, before the entry into the Promised Land. Perhaps this earliest passing on of priesthood functions via lineage had to do with the necessity of learning the art of using and interpreting the Urim and Thummim. If so, it involved passing on a skill from father to son. The many biblical references to the establishment of Aaron and his seed and the Levitical succession to priesthood clearly demonstrate that by this time, such a custom was fully institutionalized.

In any event, early established priesthoods are noted historically at the sanctuaries of Shiloh and Dan during the time of the judges. But apparently they did not serve sacrificial functions. Continuing down through this period (the fourteenth through the twelfth centuries B.C.E.), it appears that all participants in the covenant had the privilege and responsibility of offering sacrifice.

During the time of the monarchy (from the eleventh to the seventh century B.C.E.), the priests continued to use the Urim and Thummim (as described in Deuteronomy 33:8); served the important function of preserving the faith, traditions, and teachings of the nation (Deuteronomy 33:9–10); served as criminal and civil judges (Deuteronomy 17:8–11, 21:5); and began to serve as officiants in offering sacrifices on behalf of the people (Deuteronomy 33:10).

By the eighth century B.C.E., although the judicial functions were continuing, there was little mention of the prophetic role being integral with the priestly role. Instead, separate isolated individuals arose as prophets. Eventually, the use of the Urim and Thummim disappeared altogether, after serving a symbolic and authoritative role only for some time. Now the greatest emphasis in the function of priesthood was on the ritualistic aspects of their acts, with great attention to purity requirements and to isolation of the sacred from the profane.

The forty-fourth chapter of Ezekiel is interesting for its insistence on unusual purity requirements. The chapter begins (vs. 2), invoking the name of the Lord as being responsible for what is about to be required. The priests are to wear linen only: wool is expressly forbidden (vss. 17 and 18), and they are forbidden to wear anything that might cause them to sweat. These garments are for temple sanctuary wear only (vs. 19) and are to be kept there. They can't let their heads be covered with long hair or be shaven, but may only trim their natural growth of hair (vs. 20). They cannot drink wine before serving the Lord (vs. 21). They cannot marry a divorcee or a widow unless her deceased husband was also a priest. Virgins of the house of Israel are otherwise required (vs. 22). They are to observe all the holy days and sabbaths, and teach that they be observed (vss. 23–24). In their judicial role, they are to follow the God-given rules (vs. 24). A priest is not to defile himself by coming near a dead body, unless it is a close relative's body; and then he is to be purified and wait seven days before serving again (vss. 25 and 26). Then he is to offer his own sin offering before doing anything else (vs. 27). In return, the priests have the privilege of living off of the offerings given to the Lord in the Lord's sanctuary, "and every dedicated thing in Israel shall be theirs" (vs. 29). Their tribe had not shared in the apportionments of land accorded the other tribes, but they were given their livelihood from the sacred offerings.

By this time, the role of the priest as officiant in the sacrifices was well established, and the teaching of tradition was equally emphasized. Indeed, it begins to appear that their ritual functions, not their judicial functions, were the focus of many regulations governing the priests. With the development of the "priestly code" and the formation of the priesthood as a holy order (see Numbers 16:1–5, 18:7 and Leviticus 21:6–8), ritualism appears to have preoccupied the attention of the ministers. Only the priests could now serve at the altar and guard the sanctity of the sanctuary. Furthermore, trespass of the sanctuary carried the penalty of death (II Chronicles 23:6–7). Many prescriptions and proscriptions now governed the daily activities of the Levites and priests.

In Chronicles, the priests, who were descendants of Aaron, were divided into twenty-four classes (I Chronicles 24:7–19). This was necessary because of the proliferation of their numbers. Apparently there was a popular saying at the time in Jerusalem that there were as many priests and Levites in the Temple as there were stones in its walls. Estimates of their numbers reached as high as 20,000, although the Chronicler himself claims there were 38,000 Levites alone, who were assistants to the priests! (See I Chronicles 23:3.)

With growth in numbers and with the evolution of time, political aspects of their condition became apparent. Discrimination occurred on the basis of one's tribe, particular family, temple-centered or dispersed service, service in high places, etc. Those who lived away from the sanctuary, and were only available for occasional and periodic service, were discriminated against by those who lived nearby and participated regularly. This was especially critical at the time of Ezekiel, when he declared that the priesthood was henceforth to be reserved for the descendants of Zadok only. Despite this, however, the descendants of Ithamar exerted enough political influence to maintain their right to officiate as well. (See I Chronicles 24:1–6 and Driver, pp. 154–155.[5] See also Herbert G. May.[6]) From time to time, the priestly environment was highly politicized.

Further evolution of priesthood functions came to include the blowing of the trumpets to signal the alarm of war or at the time of the new moon. But it also eventually developed into a separate class whose function was to provide music at the temple.

> All these were the sons of Heman the king's seer in the words of God, to lift up the horn. And God gave to Heman fourteen sons and three daughters. All these were under the hands of their father for song in the house of the Lord, with cymbals, psalteries, and harps, for the service of the house of God.... So the number of them, with their brethren that were instructed in the songs of the Lord, even all that were cunning, was two hundred fourscore and eight. And they cast lots...as well the small as the great, the teacher as the scholar.—I Chronicles 25:5–8

Of interest also, if taken literally, is the reference in this passage to the daughters of Heman having place in the musicians' order of priesthood in the temple. This may be one of the first scriptural references to women serving in the priesthood.

Given all of the foregoing, it is apparent there was an evolution of service functions in the sacramental office. Beginning with the right and responsibility to offer sacrifice resting upon all the faithful, changes gradually were incorporated that not only limited *who* might have the right and authority to so function, but also *where* such sacrifices should occur (during certain eras, at Jerusalem only), and with *what* attention to purity they should offer sacrifice. We also note another significant change: the prophetic function, which originally inhered in the priests, eventually evolved into a separate class of ministers, whose designation was more mystical or spiritual than formal and hereditary, and whose function often appeared to be to reform the excesses of the priests or of royalty.

These changes occurred as a result of a growing complexity in their daily life and in their relations with their neighbors. They came in response to the compelling thrust of their understanding of the divine will, set in the context of their history and destiny as a people. With greater numbers of priests, whose inheritance and livelihood were in the form of the rewards of sacred service rather than portions of land, it became necessary to find something distinctive for them to do. This made it possible for ministers to specialize and created the need to qualify oneself before being permitted to serve.

Two Models for Priestly Ministry

It was into the mainstream of Jewish culture that Jesus was born. It is hard for us, at this distance, to appreciate just how great this influence was, both in support of his ministry and also in opposition to it. It was because of those differences, and not despite them, that Jesus was a popular minister. Without attacking individuals, Jesus could demonstrate the folly of Jewish society and Judaism, causing the people to catch a glimpse of what freedoms lay ahead for them in following his teachings.

Much that Jesus represented was a break with their history, tradition, and contemporary practices. He frequently said, "Ye have heard it said of old...but I say unto you...." His gospel was a new departure, and the "Good News" was to be carried by individuals of different authority to serve different functions.

The New Testament is literally that—it is a witness of something totally new and different. This is not only true with regard to the nature of Jesus' life, ministry, and teachings; it is equally true with reference to priesthood's nature and ministry. With the advent of Jesus, new concepts of the roles of leaders were taught and exemplified.

In the traditional Hebrew pattern, leaders were a professional class of society. They were priests of a particular lineage who were chosen to serve as intermediaries between God and humanity. But in Christianity, *all* were called to serve as ministers to one another in Jesus' stead. This universal call was symbolized as a call to membership in the body of Christ. The early saints shared in Christ's ministry because they felt they were integrated into a body of believers that sought to replicate the life and teachings of their Master. This was in dramatic contrast to the patriarchal society in which the church appeared, and at variance as well with the norms of Roman social organization. Instead of being related in a hierarchical relationship connoting superiority to some and inferiority to others, as members of one body, each member had equal importance with every other member of the body.

The original thrust of Christianity was to elevate all the believers to have communion with the Lord Jesus through his own intermediary, the Holy Spirit. In this there were strong elements of equality before God and before one another. The equality announced in Jesus' gospel had implications for differences of national origin, race, gender, and slavery. The New Testament clearly identified Gentiles as well as Jews for calling to priesthood service. The slave as well as the free was to be permitted to serve, though subject to permission by the slave's master. (See Ephesians 6:5–9, Colossians 3:22–23, Titus 2:9–10, I Peter 2:18–21.) As Apostle Paul stated the situation in I Corinthians 12:13:

> For by one Spirit are we all baptized into one body, whether we be Jews or Gentiles, whether we be bond or free; and have been all made to drink into one Spirit.

And again, to the Galatians he said:

> For ye are all the children of God by faith in Jesus Christ.... There is neither Jew nor Greek, there is neither bond nor free, there is neither male nor female; for ye are all one in Christ Jesus.—Galatians 3:26, 28

Equality in the early Christian Church is not merely hinted at. It is outspokenly published by its chief proponents, including Apostle Paul.

Jesus taught that God cares for the entirety of nature: a single sparrow, the lilies of the fields, the individual hairs of one's head. Such loving care is to be reflected in the lives of the disciples as well as the Master. In terms of governance, it suggests qualities that may be identified with democracy as we understand it. Such democratic relationships are seen in the way the saints related with one another and how they decided various issues.

For example, early in the book of Acts, a meeting of about 120 of the saints is described (Acts 1:15–26). From among the spiritual leaders of the young church, there were two nominees, one of whom was selected to be numbered among the apostles, not by revelation, but by a ballot vote after congregational prayer for divine insight. Such an important decision was placed in the hands of the members as a whole and not reserved to a select few from among a priestly class. Those who were privileged to have been called and ordained to serve the Master did not place themselves apart from the people they served.

Judaism, however, held fast to the importance of the role of the priests and high priests as spiritual intermediaries for the common people before God. These specialized ministers would represent the people to God and God to the people. There were strong elements of theocracy (rule by God through divinely appointed leaders) resident within Judaism and Jewish civil life, despite the Roman occupation. At Jesus' trial before Pilate and during the ensuing events, it became clear just how much authority they possessed, even under Roman domination. They were powerful enough to persuade a Roman government to cede its authority over Jesus to them, and to sway a population to wish the death of the one whom they had only recently proclaimed "king" with loud hosannas.

The New Testament church saw priesthood develop from the traditional Old Testament model into altogether new images and functions for ministry. Although the writer of the letter to the Hebrews appears to develop bridges between the Old Testament priesthood and the New Testament ministerial roles and functions, it is clearly in the context of a major departure from the established Jewish forms and functions of priesthood. His purpose is to link people of Jewish heritage with a new, radically open and progressive way of life.

Jesus' lifestyle was contagious. It was the role of a self-sacrificing servant who served for the sake of others. And others were not only *called* to emulate him, they *wanted* to. There is, therefore, a major distinction between the leadership roles found in the Old Testament—of a priesthood that stood between God and humanity—and the New Testament image of leaders who, like Jesus, came from among the people and who stood with them.

The various Christian churches have each accepted one or the other of these two traditions and have institutionalized it as their own experience. The Catholic, Orthodox, and Mormon positions appear primarily to be oriented toward the Old Testament intermediary model for priesthood; the New Testament servant role is the preferred model for much of Protestantism.

Ordinations and Offices

The record is not clear about Jesus having ordained the various offices of priesthood in the New Testament. There is, however, testimony in the Gospels that implies that Jesus ordained the twelve disciples to the function of apostle. The word "ordain" appears only twice in the King James and Inspired Versions of the Gospels. Mark 3:13 says, "And he ordained twelve..." but it does not call them apostles. The other reference is in John 15:16. Speaking to the disciples, Jesus says, "Ye have not chosen me, but I have chosen you, and ordained you, that ye should go and bring forth fruit...." Indeed, there is no single reference that links together the facts of divine calling, formal ordination, and the specific function of apostle. Mark 3:13 links calling and ordination, and Matthew 10:2 and Luke 6:13 link calling and apostleship.

There is no serious doubt about the twelve disciples having been chosen and ordained, and their service being that of apostles. But the lack of specific data linking calling, ordination, and apostolic office in the four Gospels does suggest that these details were not as important or significant to the saints of that day as they are to us today.

The only additional set of officers mentioned in the Gospels are "other seventy," cited in Luke 10:1. These missionaries were "appointed" by Jesus. They may also have been ordained, although this is not stated in Luke. They were "sent" by Jesus as advance agents to prepare the people for Jesus' own ministry when he would come their way. They were to visit in the homes of the people, receive their hospitality gratefully, share the gospel message, and heal the sick (including casting out demons). After their first ministries, they reported the results of their successes with joy (Luke 10:18). Other than the ordination of the apostles and the "appointment" of the seventy, there appears to have been little other formal organization in the early church during Jesus' lifetime.

We may speculate, with some degree of probability, as to the reasons why other priesthood offices are not included in the very early years of the church Jesus founded. First, in its earliest times, the church needed, more than any other function, the ministry of witness. Apostles (messengers who are free to travel, to be sent) and other missionaries (the seventy) should normally be needed in the early years of the expansion of a body of believers. There was strong need for their gifts in the enlisting of new members and the establishing of congregations. Other offices could come later, when their roles would be necessary to the development of a growing church. When these new offices came, they represented, for the most part, a departure from the traditional roles of priesthood as it was known among the Jews.

But perhaps the most compelling reason why other priesthood offices were not immediately instituted by Jesus is because they were not required. Ministries that later would be assumed by specific priesthood office could be carried by anyone holding the office of member when the church was small enough that larger structural forms were unnecessary. Congregations were small, small enough to meet in believers' homes. The homes themselves were small and could not have accommodated large numbers.

The congregations were rather like extended families that cared for one another's needs. They met to pray, to sing hymns, to share the good news, to strengthen one another, and, after Jesus was no longer with them, to observe the Lord's supper. Those who were Jews still attended worship services at the temple and in the synagogues. This afforded them opportunity to testify of the Lord Jesus and to bring new converts into their own fellowship. During his lifetime, Jesus recognized the authority of the Jewish priesthood, and we can only assume that the early disciples did also, following his example.

Shortly after Jesus' ascension, we have this view of how the early church functioned:

> ...they continued steadfastly in the apostles' doctrine and fellowship, and in breaking of bread, and in prayers...and many wonders and signs were done by the apostles. And all that believed were together, and had all things common; and sold their possessions and goods, and parted them to all men, as every man had need. And they, continuing daily with one accord in the temple, and breaking bread from house to house, did eat their meat with gladness and singleness of heart, praising God, and having favor with all the people....—Acts 2:42–47

With small groups of saints meeting in various homes wherever the work was organized, a great informality prevailed. Their isolation was avoided by whoever might be traveling among them, especially those ministers called to do so. From time to time they would be privileged to receive the ministry of an apostle. They may not have continued to receive ministry from the seventy missionaries chosen by Jesus, for there is but the one reference in Luke, and nothing further about them in the apostolic church scriptures. Other missionaries are named as associates of the Twelve in their labors, but none of them are called "seventy," nor is the title cited again.

There was a great deal of pragmatism at work as the church grew and grew and outgrew its former organizational forms. But the ministry of the members was such that tasks needing to be done could be done, in most cases not requiring ordination, by any member. The small congregations that began in the homes—and later due to oppression were found in the catacombs—did not require a full roster of priesthood offices. Probably the average member in the congregation keenly felt his or her calling to Christ and to Christian service. They were ready to respond in whatever way the Holy Spirit prompted their ministry, according to the circumstances and devotion of particular members. Justifiably it may be said that the chief office in the very early church was the office of member.

Within a few decades, as the church grew in complexity, expanding its frontiers into many nations and cultures, and as the apostles were extended over vast territories with little means of communication and travel, other officers were greatly needed.

Elders had existed in the Jewish synagogues, and this role was easily accepted as the Holy Spirit prompted the apostles to ordain other ministers. There were other officers serving in synagogues of this period: head (or ruler) of the synagogue (Nicodemus held this office—John 3:1; as did Jairus—Luke 8:42); father of the synagogue; mother of the synagogue; priest (*hiereus'*). In the case of temple priests (*hiereus'*), because of their lineage, after the temple's destruction they were sometimes accorded the honor of serving in some of the synagogue ministerial roles, although their order, as such, had ceased to function.

None of the other synagogue offices were included in the early Christian Church except that of elder. Paul and Barnabas, on a ministerial visit to Derbe, "ordained them elders in every church..." (Acts 14:23).

By the time Paul wrote his letter to the saints at Philippi, there were bishops and deacons giving leadership there (Philippians 1:1). In a letter to Timothy, Paul suggests it was appropriate for individuals to desire, and perhaps seek, to serve in priesthood offices (I Timothy 3:1). He set out the criteria for someone desiring to serve as a bishop. Bishops, as overseers, presided with authority over larger congregations. Evangelists were needed to help in the preaching of the gospel and often accompanied the apostles into their fields.

During this period of rapid expansion, the fledgling church saw its task to have dual functions: witnessing and ministering to human need. We are, therefore, not surprised at the recognition of physical as well as spiritual needs. What began on an "as needed" basis with a small group of saints eventually required organized efforts. In the local congregation, if there were poor requiring support, those who had surplus could sell some of their possessions or goods to provide for the less fortunate saints. But by the time the apostle Paul wrote his epistle to the Romans, already a linkage was needed to bring the support from believers in one country to bear on the poverty of those of another nation.

> ...now I go unto Jerusalem to minister unto the saints. For it hath pleased them of Macedonia and Achaia to make a certain contribution for the poor saints which are at Jerusalem.—Romans 15:25-26

Within a relatively short time, such needs demanded ongoing attention, more than an itinerant apostle could provide. Problems developed when the poor of one area appeared to be overlooked. It was probably not discrimination but a matter of communication and distribution, for the early saints certainly gave the impression of wanting to care for the needs of all segments of the church. Notice how this situation is described in Acts 6:1-7.

> And in those days, when the number of the disciples was multiplied, there arose a murmuring of the Grecians against the Hebrews, because their widows were neglected in the daily ministration. Then the twelve called the multitude of the disciples unto them, and said, It is not reason that we should leave the word of God, and serve [*diakone'o*] tables. Wherefore, brethren, look ye out among you seven men of honest report, full of the Holy Ghost and wisdom, whom we may appoint [*kathis'temi*, translated "ordain" in three other New Testament passages] over this business. But we will give ourselves continually to prayer, and to the ministry of the word. And the saying pleased the whole multitude;

and they chose Stephen, a man full of faith and of the Holy Ghost, and Philip, and Prochorus, and Nicanor, and Timon, and Parmenas, and Nicolas a proselyte of Antioch; whom they set before the apostles; and when they had prayed, they laid their hands on them. And the word of God increased; and the number of the disciples multiplied in Jerusalem greatly; and a great company of the priests [*hiereus'*] were obedient to the faith.

Wisely the apostles did not wish to appear negligent in their own evangelistic calling by spending too much of their valuable time in caring for the poor. Others who were perhaps even more gifted in such a ministry could readily assume this role. Here was their procedure: the apostles informed a large conference of saints that they would leave to the conference the selection of seven capable ministers to provide a unique ministry to the poor, avoiding the slighting of any who had need. Note the egalitarian relationships between the apostles and the members. Democratic procedures were employed rather than hierarchic or authoritarian power. The conference approved this recommendation and chose seven godly men. After prayer, the Twelve ordained them through the laying on of hands. And the church was blessed: the witness was increased, the number of disciples grew, even including some joining the church who had been temple priests.

To what office were these seven ordained? We cannot be certain. We may have a clue within the text itself. When the apostles referred to the task as being "serving tables," this may have been less pejorative and more descriptive than we now imagine. The verb "to serve" [*diakone'o*] has the same root as its noun [*diak'onos*], meaning "deacon." Therefore the phrase could potentially be translated "deaconing" tables. However, one of these brethren, Philip, was also called "evangelist" in Acts 21:8. The seven evangelists or deacons would have traveled in the midst of the congregations from time to time, which may account for the reference to Philip as an evangelist, for he certainly would have preached the gospel wherever he went. Functionally, their labor agrees more with our present-day notions of the role of a deacon than that of an evangelist. This only illustrates how difficult it is for us to see the past with our modern eyes.

In each case, these words are descriptive of the roles and functions they were to serve. Consequently, due to the increased breadth and depth of ministry that was called for when the gospel was being shared beyond the temple or synagogue, most of these are functions that were not thought of or foreseen in the traditional Jewish religion. We ought not, therefore, to be surprised that there is not too much office-related resemblance between the Old Testament priesthood and New Testament ministries. After all, the call of Christ was to enter into relationships of ministry with all sorts of people, including many who had not been a part of the experience of Judaism.

Because these functions were served for the sake of people in the midst of life as they lived it, priesthood innovations were directly related to the lifestyle and culture of the people. In the New Testament, we do not see a concept of priesthood that came out of eternity or even as a legacy from Judaism, seeming to have little relevance to life as it was lived by the current generation.

On the contrary, the actual functioning of the priesthood, and consequently its structures, was directly related to the salvation process for people in the midst of human life. Its staying power and its link with eternity was that its origin was in the eternal love of an eternal God who holds forth the promise of eternal life for humanity. The saving ministries that God inspired in people were the result of the Holy Spirit which moved among them and motivated them to service. Communication with God created in them a sense of calling to which they readily responded. Good, Spirit-led ministry was the effect of such a cause.

This ministry originally was performed without priesthood office by the members of the body. The functioning of the "office of member" is clearly discerned. Saints of early days were much like latter-day Saints: there were members, and then there were *members*. For many people, the new life in Christ was so liberating that they were free to serve the Lord with all their heart, soul, and mind. They understood what it meant to function *ex officio* or officially as a member of the body of Christ. Their calling to serve came with the authority of the Holy Spirit received in confirmation through the laying on of hands.

Such members, both in ancient times and today, hold the "office of member" and serve faithfully in it. And then there are others who are members—some in name only, some who are "lukewarm" (like John the Revelator's Laodiceans), and others who bring reproach on the body. All these are members and are worthy of ministry and acceptance, but all do not serve in the office of member. Joseph Smith's reference to the "office of...member" in Doctrine and Covenants 104:5, if taken literally, extends the listing of priesthood offices to include the office of member.

Perhaps not everyone is called to priesthood offices requiring ordination, but the potential to serve in the office of member is available to everyone who has been baptized in Christ. This was apparently also the case in the New Testament church. We find the prophetic descriptions of the contemporary congregations made by John the Revelator to be so similar to qualities of membership exhibited by congregations of our own time that comparisons are hard to avoid. The early Christian Church, too, had some who were nominally members and others who felt called to serve in the "office of member."

By the time of the later New Testament writers, already there were traces of the institutionalization of some functions into priesthood offices. To acknowledge the truth of the situation, we need only to be aware that the very names used to identify the priesthood roles were themselves functionally descriptive. Whereas they have been adapted into English in most cases rather than translated, we may simply return to the original Greek to learn that these words are less like the names of offices and more appropriately like functions.

For example, the term "deacon" comes from the Greek word *diak'onos* which means "servant." Instead of translating the term as a name for the office, we have simply adapted the Greek word into an English form and used it as a name.

The term "teacher" (*didas'kalos*) has been translated into English, and, therefore, denotes one who serves the function of teaching.

The English word "priest" in fact is derived etymologically from the Greek word *presbu'teros*. However, *presbu'teros* is correctly translated "elder" in English, and it is from this same word that we get the English word "presbyter." Some dictionaries, therefore, list both "priest" and "elder" as appropriate meanings for "presbyter." As a result, in the Restoration movement there may be a confusing of the terms "priest" and "elder" by virtue of their common origin in the same Greek word, if it is suggested that both offices existed in the primitive Christian Church. The reason why we have both offices in the RLDS Church is due to latter-day revelation and not because they both existed as such in the New Testament church.

The word used to denote the priest who served in the Jewish temple is the Greek word *hiereus'*, which literally means an officiant of the temple (*hieron'*). The New Testament church included some who had previously been temple priests and were now converted Christians. But they no longer functioned in their office of temple priest and served as any other member of the body of Christ. Some, like Saul of Tarsus, were ordained to other offices within the Christian faith.

The term "bishop" comes from the Greek word *epis'kopos*, which means "overseer," and thus the New Testament bishops were those who had the oversight of the congregations of the church. This term is used in the first chapter of Acts, when a new apostle was selected to replace Judas Iscariot. In presenting the situation before the conference of the saints, recommending that someone be selected for this office, Peter referred to phrases from Psalm

69: "His bishopric (*episkopē'*) let another take." In I Timothy 3:1, this same word is translated "office of a bishop." But the word's basic meaning is "overseer." It was not the apostles' intention to ordain a bishop when they ordained Mathias: he was to serve with the other eleven apostles. But Judas' stewardship or office was to be given to Mathias, who replaced him.

There appears to have been a time during the creation of the New Testament writings when terms for function and office were used interchangeably, or the term was descriptively related with a function. For example, when Paul spoke to the elders at Ephesus, he called them *epis'kopos*, meaning that they had oversight of the flock and not that they were ordained bishops. In the course of his exhortation, he said,

> Take heed therefore unto yourselves, and to all the flock, over the which the Holy Ghost hath made you overseers [Greek: *epis'kopos*, which is usually translated in the New Testament by the English word "bishop"], to feed the church of God, which he hath purchased with his own blood. For I know this, that after my departing shall grievous wolves enter in among you, not sparing the flock. Also of your own selves shall men arise, speaking perverse things, to draw away disciples after them.—Acts 20:28–30

The term "apostle" comes from the word *apos'tolos*, which means "messenger" or "those who are sent."

The term "evangelist" comes from the word *euanggelistēs'*, which denotes one who shares the evangel, the gospel.

The term "prophet" comes from the word *prophē'tēs*, which means one who tells forth the word of God. It, therefore, could appropriately be translated in English to mean either one who foretells (a prophet who provides the will of God in advance) or one who tells forth (a prophet or preacher who provides the will of God for today). Judas Barsabas and Silas are called prophets in Acts 15:32 specifically because they "exhorted the brethren with many words, and confirmed them." But it is likely they possessed the gift of prophecy.

Women Disciples

Jesus was at ease in the home of Martha, Mary, and Lazarus. They were more than close friends. Their ties were greater than kinship ties, so significantly involved in each others' lives did they become. Later, Jesus would weep at Lazarus' death and the sorrow of his sisters—and Jesus would be moved so deeply that he would raise him from his tomb to life again with his sisters.

Martha had learned her role well. As a good Jewish woman, she gave great care to their household and was an especially good hostess when Jesus was the guest. But it irked her that Mary did not give her a hand with all the important chores that needed attention. Martha had extended the invitation: Jesus was her guest. But Mary spent all the time talking with Jesus, and Martha had to do all the cooking and serving alone. She undoubtedly felt cheated and put-upon by her sister, on whom she had depended for help. It was certainly their shared role as hostesses to attend to this great rabbi's needs. Customs of hospitality and the cultural role of women in Jewish society demanded a certain task-related function of these two sisters.

However, Mary had other things on her mind. She "also sat at Jesus' feet, and heard his words."

In Jewish society—in which women were forbidden from participating in the synagogue with the men but were isolated behind curtains in the women's gallery where they were neither permitted to be seen nor heard—it was not the norm for a woman to be interested in such a manly thing as the theological lessons Rabbi Jesus might teach. But she also sat at Jesus' feet: she wanted to hear his teaching.

When Martha thought to reproach Mary by enlisting Jesus to remind her of her womanly duties, Jesus surprised Martha by fully supporting Mary's choice (Luke 10:39–43). He explained, "Martha, you are a person of great care, and you carry a concern for many things—all of which is very good. But there really is only one thing that is essential, and Mary has chosen it, and it will not be taken from her." Jesus appears to be more concerned about respecting Mary's freedom of choice and her decision to enter into significant questions about the meaning of life than to merely reinforce society's notions about gender-related roles for women. It was appropriate—indeed, it was the better part—to choose to become an intelligent, studious, responsive disciple of the Lord.

Women played important roles in these early years of the Christian Church. Jesus was just as ready to offer his ministry to a woman or girl as a man or boy. Without discrimination, he touched the lives of all who heard him. His parables called to mind feminine images as well as masculine. His appeal for people to follow him and enter into the ministries of his kingdom was as great for the women as for the men. And there are noteworthy women mentioned by the Gospel writers—women who were noticed because of their direct involvement in Jesus' life and ministry.

Similarly, the book of Acts names many women among the chief church members and saints. That women were deeply involved in the early church cannot be denied, but it is disputed whether or not their roles were priesthood roles. Historically, it is known that there was a special order of widows, and within the New Testament there are evidences of their existence. Widows could become a part of an organization that permitted their unique home ministry within the church.

At Joppa, Tabitha (or Dorcas, as she was also called) may have been one of such a group, as well as the widows who mourned her death, described in Acts 9:36–42. It is noteworthy that the writer distinguishes between "the saints" and "the widows" in this story, as if their role was significant enough to make this distinction. In his letter to Timothy, Paul describes this servant organization:

> Let not a widow be taken into the number under threescore years old, having been the wife of one man, well reported of for good works; if she have brought up children, if she have lodged strangers, if she have washed the saints' clothes, if she have relieved the afflicted, if she have diligently followed every good work.—I Timothy 5:9–10

Other women served the Lord and the church in other ways. Phoebe is referred to as "servant" in Romans 16:1. However, the masculine, not the feminine, form of the word is used: *diak'onos*. Because the same word is also translated "deacon" and "minister" in other places in the New Testament, we would be just as warranted in translating this passage to read "deacon" (or "deaconess" as some translators have done). It is the masculine form of the word which is most puzzling, for whether "servant," "minister," or "deacon," the feminine form would have been more appropriate if agreement with gender were important. If it is a priesthood office that is intended, and if the writer thought the word to have masculine gender, then he may have been justified in using the masculine form with a woman holding the office of deacon. But it is, nonetheless, puzzling why the masculine was used.

Whether or not Phoebe was a deacon, we learn from other historical sources that deaconesses were known in the New Testament church. Corroborating historical reference is found in a letter of Pliny to Trajan (109 C.E.). From this early tradition, deaconesses have continued in the Greek Orthodox Church down to the present day. Although the term "deaconess" is used in Canon 19 of the Nicene Council (325 C.E.), and by the Archbishop of York (732–766 C.E.), and by the Bishop of Exeter (1050–1072 C.E.), the consecrated office of deaconess did not survive in the Roman Catholic Church, and hence was generally lost to early Protestantism as well.

It appears that there may also have been female elders. (See Luke 2:36 and I Timothy 5:1–2.) The writers of the New Testament included female elders (*presbu'tera*) as a regular part of the body of the saints. There is a linguistic problem with regard to *presbu'teros/presbu'tera,* in that the same word is used both in its masculine and feminine forms. It could always be translated to mean "elderly man" and "elderly woman" or "male elders" and "female elders" or according to context, occasionally one way and then the other. However, the last alternative is ours only if it was so currently used in the cultural context of the New Testament church. If one were to suppose that the male term "elders" usually or always meant a priesthood office, then we are almost obliged to interpret the female form of the noun to mean that women held the same office.

From evidence within the New Testament, it also appears that women held other prominent positions. Notice these several names, and how they are respected by Apostle Paul:

> I commend unto you Phoebe our sister, which is a servant of the church which is at Cenchrea; that you receive her in the Lord, as becometh saints, and that ye assist her in whatsoever business she hath need of you; for she hath been a succorer of many, and of myself also. Greet Priscilla and Aquila, my helpers in Christ Jesus; who have for my life laid down their own necks; unto whom not only I give thanks, but also all the churches of the Gentiles. Likewise greet the church that is in their house.... Greet Mary, who bestowed much labor on us. Salute Andronicus and Junia, my kinsmen, and my fellow prisoners, who are of note among the apostles, who also were in Christ before me.—Romans 16:1–7

And Paul goes on to name other women and men with whom he wanted to share his greetings and appreciation.

This last reference to Junia is important, in that it suggests she may have held the office of apostle. According to some prominent church leaders, this interpretation is valid. Chrysostom lived from 347 to 407 C.E., a renowned church leader in the period before the darkness of spirit usually associated with the Middle Ages had pervaded the church. In "Homily XXXI" from his *Homilies on the Acts of the Apostles and the Epistle to the Romans*, Chrysostom says,

> For the women of those days were more spirited than lions, sharing with the Apostles their labors for the Gospel's sake. In this way they went travelling with them, and also performed all other ministries....

And then, with specific reference to Romans 16:7, referring to Andronicus and Junia, he says,

> ...indeed to be apostles at all is a great thing. But even to be amongst these of note, just consider what a great encomium this is! But they were of note owing to their works, to their achievements. Oh! how great is the devotion of this woman, that she should be even counted worthy of the appellation of apostle![7]

The French Catholic father Lagrange comments about this couple:

> ...Jerome and Ambrosiaster, as well as Chrysostom, were able to regard Junia as a woman apostle.... Andronicus and Junia would thus be husband and wife... When Andronicus and Junia were in captivity with Paul, that's what we don't know. They were... what all the ancients understood: "distinguished among the apostles," and it is in fact the only meaning possible.[8]

C. E. B. Cranfield, professor of theology at the University of Durham, also said,

> ...it is surely right to assume that the person referred to was a woman (with Chrysostom, col. 670, and Lagrange, p. 366).... Most probably Andronicus and Junia were husband and wife.... [This passage] has sometimes been understood as meaning "outstanding in the eyes of the apostles...." While this must be judged grammatically possible, it is much more probable—we might well say, virtually certain—that the words mean "outstanding among the apostles," that is, "outstanding in the group who may be designated apostles," which is the way in which it was understood by the patristic commentators (it would seem, without exception).... That Paul should not only include a woman (on the view taken above)

among the apostles but actually describe her, together with Andronicus, as outstanding among them, is highly significant evidence (along with the importance he accords in this chapter to Phoebe, Prisca, Mary, Tryphaena, Tryphosa, Persis, the mother of Rufus, Julia and the sister of Nereus) of the falsity of the widespread and stubbornly persistent notion that Paul had a low view of women....[9]

There may have been other women, holding other offices of the priesthood in these early times. The record we have is fragmentary and subject to interpretation by the various authorities, who do not always agree. But we are aware from internal evidence that the New Testament writers used the same Greek word (only modified by the feminine ending) as a label for the functional service of women who served as prophetesses (*prophē'tis*).

Bernadette J. Brooten, in a program of Judaic studies at Brown University, published a book titled *Women Leaders in the Ancient Synagogue*. It is the published form of her doctoral thesis and was found worthy of acceptance into the Brown Judaic Studies. In the book's Introduction she states:

> It is my thesis that women served as leaders in a number of synagogues during the Roman and Byzantine periods. The evidence for this consists of nineteen Greek and Latin inscriptions in which women bear the titles of "head of the synagogue," "leader," "elder," "mother of the synagogue," and "priestess." These inscriptions range in date from 27 B.C.E. to perhaps the sixth century C.E. and in provenance from Italy to Asia Minor, Egypt and Palestine. While new discoveries make this a growing corpus of material, a number of the inscriptions have been known to scholars for some time.[10]

She then proceeds to make a detailed analysis of each inscription. These are archeological finds, usually associated with burials and sarcophagi. They give such data as names, dates, and honors, functions, or offices held by the women. It is in this context that some Jewish women were found to have played important leadership roles in synagogues of the period, certainly consisting of priesthood responsibility. These are hard evidences of Jewish women sometimes carrying ministerial and leadership roles which usually have been assumed to have been held only by men. They support the parallel contemporary involvement of women in the early Christian Church. Brooten calls attention to this.

One inscription is of unusual interest for members of the RLDS Church. It is in Latin and makes reference to a woman by the name of Alexsandra. "Here lies Elexsanra [sic], fatheress [sic], who lived approximately (. . .). Peace!" The Latin term used, translated by Bernadette Brooten as "fatheress," is an unusual form of a Latin word, *pateressa*—somewhat akin to another English hybrid word, "patriarchess."

Brooten also mentions a more recent discovery by Martin Hengel of an inscription from Aphrodisias in Caria, dating from the third or fourth century. It refers to a woman by the name of Jael who is called *prostates*, meaning "presiding officer, patron, guardian." Her son, Josua, is also mentioned as *archon*, "head or ruler of the synagogue." This same noun, *prostat'is*, is translated in the King James version of Romans 16:2 to be "succorer" with regard to Phoebe, rather an equivalent to "patron." However, given the context in which Paul asks the other members to "assist her in whatsoever business she hath need of you," it would seem that a more authoritative role for Phoebe may have been indicated. The Greek verb *prostas'so* (having the same root as the noun *prostat'is*) is translated six times by the word "command" in the New Testament. Phoebe may have borne considerable responsibility in her church at Cenchrea.

Wolves among the Flock

While the early New Testament church was open, Spirit-directed, and led by gifted people who freely used their gifts without restrictions of polity and hierarchy, the postapostolic church soon had to deal with the problems of a growing institution. False doctrines and their proponents required decisive action by administrators. This was not necessarily a new problem. Paul and his contemporaries left a record in the New Testament of some of the difficulties they had already encountered.

Immature but ardent witnesses, who needed more instruction themselves, left a trail of partially converted saints behind them (Acts 18:24–19:7). There was division in the church over the question of circumcision (Acts 15). Paul had to deal with exorcists who misrepresented the Lord and the church (Acts 19:13–16) and with a sorcerer/false prophet who sought "to turn away [Sergius Paulus] from the faith…" and "to pervert the right ways of the Lord" (see Acts 13:6–12).

But it was after Paul had lived through these experiences that he admonished the elders at Ephesus. He said that following his departure to imprisonment and death, "grievous wolves" would enter in among them and that they should "take heed unto the flock." After the passing of the early apostles and without their charismatic leadership, these problems only took on new forms and greater severity. Oppression from opposing cultures and governments created a necessity for solidarity in well-integrated congregations. The need for stability, security, and permanence virtually forced the church to move into more structured models with authority figures empowered to act for the good of the body.

When they did this, they quite naturally chose organizational models that came out of their heritage. For many congregations, that was a Jewish heritage. Bernadette Brooten suggests this relationship, citing Epiphanius of Salamis (ca. 315–403 C.E.) as a supporting reference. Epiphanius describes a group of dissenting fringe-Christians, Ebionites, who came from a Jewish origin and employed certain Jewish organizational structures in their congregational life.[11]

While the Ebionites mentioned by Epiphanius are not necessarily typical of the saints of that period, their action to rely on time-proven authorities and structures, taken when group integrity is a critical issue, may be very typical. For the majority of the congregations, the forms of organization were probably Old Testament ones, modified with elements from the Greco-Roman world.

Once again, the ability of the common people to have direct access to God in worship experiences gradually became subordinate to the intermediary of a professional clergy. A priestly class of society stood again between the people and God. And the officers of religion began anew to function as rulers, judges, and mediators of the word. Eventually, priesthood alone held virtually all the keys of access to God and spiritual matters, and the common people were encouraged to recognize the status and authority of their clergy. Thus the hierarchy of the Christian Church could be appropriately compared with the Jewish hierarchy, as Clement of Rome did.

By the second century the ecclesiastical hierarchy was established. A sharp line of delineation between the body of members and the priesthood, the laity and the clergy, was now apparent. Increasingly the ministers were seen as standing in the stead of Christ, and as God's representatives on earth. These symbols and images reinforced the earlier male dominance already present in Judaism. It was further supported by the militant Roman image of Christianity conquering the world in the sign of the cross.

The concept that "ye are all one in Christ Jesus—there is neither Jew nor Greek, there is neither bond nor free, there is neither male nor female" (Galatians 3:28) had now given way to the practice that the church was, in fact, divided into priesthood and members, clergy and laity, leaders and followers, the powerful and the powerless—no matter how necessary or culturally determined the division. Once again, we see the people of God, so soon after the freshness of their immediate revelatory experience with Christ, adapting the institutional church and its structures to the demands of life in the real world confronting them. The church, for better or for worse, had entered into the give-and-take of a three-way dialogue with God, one another, and the world.

Priesthood in the Reorganization

During the first week of May 1866, the First Presidency and the Council of Twelve met in the home of Bishop Israel L. Rogers in Kendall County, Illinois. The recent U.S. Civil War had left unanswered certain questions regarding who could appropriately hold priesthood office.

Black men had already been ordained in the Restoration movement, so there was no need for new precedents. But that is all they were, a few precedents: there never had been many blacks called and ordained. Slavery had been an issue in Missouri during periods of discrimination against the Latter Day Saints who usually were antislavery in their sentiments. But there now seemed to be political and social pressure to proceed in ordaining black men.

In the past, such calls were processed on the basis of equal standing with men of other races, and a part of that consideration had to do with education, ability to minister, acceptability as a minister, and related questions. There is always an element of human subjectivity involved in the initiation of calls to ministry. More than ever in the years immediately following the war, there were environmental constraints requiring some formal decision as to how the church would approach this matter. The Council of Twelve raised the issue before the joint meeting, and the group entered into a period of fasting and prayer.

It was in this context that the revelation later adopted as Section 116 was received by President Joseph Smith III, and he shared it with the brethren in council. The Council of Twelve unanimously approved the revelation.

Joseph, in bringing spiritual guidance to the church, did not hesitate to place it in the context of the U.S. Civil War and its aftermath. The attitudes of people and the laws of the land had a direct bearing on the content of the message. They also affected access to priesthood for some categories of men and the effective scope of their ministry.

The document said: "Be not hasty in ordaining men of the Negro race to offices in my church, for verily I say unto you, All are not acceptable unto me as servants…and there are some who are chosen instruments to be ministers to their own race. Be ye content, I the Lord have spoken it" (Doctrine and Covenants 116:4).

To see priesthood in the light of Old and New Testament history frees us to examine the question of who may hold priesthood in the context of cultural considerations. This has been the historical experience of the church. Priesthood, as we have so far seen it, is not of some universal essence that may be universally applied. Rather, it is an opportunity and responsibility extended to some by a divine call, to serve the purposes of God in the current historical situation, and in light of the many cross-currents within the social order.

In 1866, some blacks were to be called, but they were not to partake of the essence of priesthood in offering ministry to all people as if they were possessors of an authoritative, divine, universal priesthood. Rather they were called to share a functional, ministerial role within a limited population drawn from their own racial type. Were blacks to have access to the priesthood? Yes, but.... And with that "but," all of the possibilities of interpretation, application, and accommodation came into play.

Twenty-seven years later, Joseph Smith III would bring to the church a broader statement, encompassing all races, cultures, women, and people of all ages and handicaps. "All are called according to the gifts of God unto them; and to the intent that all may labor together, let [them]...labor together with God for the accomplishment of the work intrusted to all" (Doctrine and Covenants 119:8b). The task belongs to everyone, under God; and everyone is called to serve. The role of member is still primary and universal, but some are called to serve in priesthood roles. When that is their calling, they share "the work intrusted to all" with every other member, without discrimination.

But priesthood does not exist in an idealistic vacuum. It is interrelated with society in culture. While the office of member is universal, the office of priesthood is not to be applied universally. It is contingent on many factors, not the least of which is the experience of the earthly, human church with the divine revelation. And, it is "according to the gifts of God unto them" that individuals are called. Factors of giftedness, divine call, cultural approbation, personal choice, and the general support of the people who are to be recipients of the ministry—all of these and many other factors have a direct bearing on priesthood and its particularity.

Priesthood Today

We are a people with a history. It tells us who we are; it gives us our identity. Individuals may, for a number of reasons, take legal action to change their names, but that does not change their identity. They are who they are, because their personality and character are a living summation of their history. When we stand figuratively or ultimately before the divine bar of justice, the Judge will not need to say, "On such-and-such a day you committed this or that sin." Our character and personality will reveal who and what we are without the necessity of reciting our entire life story. That history is well-written into our very being.

And so it is with the church. We are a summation of our history. If we were to deny our history, we would only be denying our own selfhood, and entering into a world of fantasy. Within our history we have many things to be proud of, and many other things (of which we are not proud) that teach us what to avoid.

Priesthood within today's church traces its history back to the earliest of times, even before recorded history. We possess as our own the heritage of Hebrew and Jewish priesthood. We are the beneficiaries of early New Testament church decisions that brought many qualities of today's priesthood to us. We are also the inheritors of priesthood traditions of the Middle Ages, the Renaissance, and the Protestant Reformation. We are the direct descendants of those who were the founders of the Restoration movement and who were "the first elders" of our ordinations. All of these together give our priesthood its identity, character, and characteristics.

Some of that composite inheritance is readily seen when we look at the roster of priesthood offices in today's church. To merely recite their names calls to mind images of the people of God of former centuries.

Patriarch	Apostle
High priest	Seventy
Priest	Evangelist
Elder	Deacon
Teacher	Bishop

Additional terms for the elective roles of "pastor" and "president" also come out of our heritage. Many of the functions we assign to these various priesthood offices have been culturally determined and continue to be so determined today.

This is a valuable trait for an international or "world" church such as we profess to be. Today's church includes rapidly growing local churches in several Third World countries where the history, culture, economy, and even language (and, therefore, patterns of thought and their processes) are greatly different from the church in a typical Western nation. Cultural accommodation for the names of priesthood offices is not only relatively easy; it brings an added sign of our international unity. For elders of a Third World church to assemble with elders from all over the world at a conference symbolizes our unity. And the local Saints in Third World countries, when utilizing priesthood terms that may be foreign to their culture, will only wear this badge of their union with an international church all the more proudly.

We should expect that using the same names for priesthood offices will not, however, limit the naturally needed cultural accommodation. For example, the duties of deacon pertaining to the care and maintenance of the church's physical properties may differ greatly from culture to culture. Thatched huts have different maintenance needs than concrete, glass, and steel structures. The duties of the office of teacher may involve certifying the appropriateness of a particular member's receiving the emblems of the Lord's Supper among the Sora tribes of India. And in a Western nation, the same office may focus more on bringing a counseling ministry to individuals recovering from addiction to alcohol or other substances.

We also should expect there to be a need for varying numbers of ministers of a given office among the various nations. Where Aaronic priesthood is perceived to be greatly needed, there will likely be greater numbers of calls to the Aaronic offices. Where the need for spiritual ministry is thought to be greater, we might expect there to be more calls to the various offices of the Melchisedec priesthood. The tendency to call and ordain fewer numbers of teachers than any other office in the Western nations during recent decades may well have cultural reasons.

Lineage is also a matter that is historically and culturally rooted in Judaism, as described in an earlier chapter. With the prevalent concept of priesthood in the Restoration being a "restoring" of earlier understandings and practices, the notion of lineage was prominent within the RLDS Church during its early years. The argument of lineage being important in priesthood succession was used by debaters who frequently confronted the issues between the Mormon and RLDS Churches because of its implications for succession in the office of prophet-president. The fact of Joseph Smith Jr.'s sons and grandsons serving in the RLDS Church was a powerful reason for supporting the value of lineage.

However, lineage as understood and practiced in Judaism never was observed in the Restoration movement. There never has been any family who, like the descendants of Aaron or Levi, were all entitled to serve in sacerdotal roles. Even the Smith family, some of whom have provided a unique and fine ministry of leadership in the RLDS Church, has never functioned in a way parallel to Aaron or Levi and their descendants. Furthermore, succession in the presidency of the church is prescribed by law in the Doctrine and Covenants. Lineage is not one of the requirements. What is required is that the successor be called by the incumbent president (Doctrine and Covenants 43:2a) through revelation (Doctrine and Covenants 99:6a), ordained (Doctrine and Covenants 43:2c) by direction of a General Conference (Doctrine and Covenants 17:17), and acknowledged by the voice of the church (Doctrine and Covenants 99:6a).

The church has been blessed by having numerous families whose descendants have carried on the tradition of priesthood ministry and service in the name of the Lord. But this has been viewed less and less as a matter of lineage, and more as a blessing and heritage.

There are precise ways in today's church for calling individuals to priesthood. Usually an elder, serving as elected pastor, initiates a call for someone within the congregation. The pastor only makes the recommendation after some light of divine inspiration has been received, because the pastor must testify that the calling has come by revelatory insight. Recommendation forms are completed by the pastor, and they are forwarded to the next higher jurisdictional officer, usually a stake or district president. This officer must also be prepared to testify as to the divinity of the call before it is approved. In districts where there is regional organization, it is the regional administrator who approves the call.

At this point, the one being called—the ordinand—is given the opportunity to hear the testimony of at least one of these officers making the recommendation. He or she frequently will have received some prompting of the Holy Spirit moving in this direction, and will not be surprised when approached and asked to accept the call. From this time on, the ordinand will be engaged in serious preparations for ministry, including the study of prescribed courses that will acquaint him or her with the duties and expectations of the office.

After these administrative approvals and the acceptance of the ordinand, the matter is brought before branch and district conferences, or a stake conference, where the people who will be the recipients of the ordinand's ministry have an opportunity to give or withhold their consent to the ordination. The ordination will be provided for by the appropriate administrative officer, and the person will be ordained by other members of the priesthood having authority.

In this procedure, several very important things occur. A revelatory experience has initiated the call. Corroborating testimony from other spiritual leaders has been received. The ordinand has a personal testimony of acceptance of the call as representing the divine will. The people, in conference session, make the final decision to approve the ordination. Both theocracy and democracy have functioned in the procedure. By the laying on of hands during the ordination, a direct line of succession in authority can be traced.

Thus the sources of authority are from "on high," from "the grass roots up," and from one's immediate supervisors and colleagues. The ordinand is surrounded by people who not only favor the ordination, but who have testified, by one means or another, that the calling is authentic, that it is God's will, and that they support him or her in their new duties.

In a practical way, there are additional expectations of a new ordinand. These are expectations that exist even before consideration of the call by the calling officer. Individuals will probably not be called to priesthood unless they attend church regularly, support the local and World Church jurisdictions financially with tithes and offerings, evidence a ministerial attitude as they serve in the office of member, demonstrate a Christian demeanor in all professional and business dealings, and abstain from social and personal habits (such as substance abuse) that would hinder and detract from service.

Some church members have the understanding that, as a former member of the Council of Twelve used to say, every able-bodied man has a potential calling to priesthood, if he is willing to prepare for and accept the call. Today that expectation would include women. Indeed, in some congregations at least, it seems that practically every truly active member, both male and female, has been called to some priesthood office or another. This creates a concern on the part of many for the unintended consequence of creating two classes of members: the priesthood and the nonpriesthood.

This division undervalues and overlooks the marvelous contributions of many people who, in the office of member, provide fine ministries in their professional and private lives away from the church environment. While many priesthood members also do this, it does not in any way diminish the importance of the unordained members' ministry. Some, through the office of member, are so busily engaged in their routine ministries that they are overlooked for priesthood calls. Many musicians and church school teachers, especially those who work with children, if they truly accept their full stewardship in that calling, do not have much time for other activities. Instead of attending midweek prayer service, for example, they may devote several hours each week in preparing for next Sunday morning's ministry—a ministry that does not require any calling beyond the calling of member.

But the truth is, many of the duties regularly performed by priesthood do not require ordination. Few of the elements of a typical worship service actually *require* that a member of the priesthood perform them. Those who hold the office of member may also provide the same ministry, if their gifts qualify them. From time to time, the unordained, occasionally even nonmembers, may serve any of the following functions:

- Offer prayers of invocation and benediction, or other special prayers
- Bring an offertory statement and/or prayer, and collect the offerings from the congregation
- Share a testimony or bring the major address ("the Word") to the congregation
- Preside over parts of or the entirety of a worship service, under the overall direction and supervision of an elder
- Lead a responsive reading, or read the scriptures or other elements of worship
- Participate in drama

These illustrations represent an almost complete list of what happens in a congregation on Sunday mornings, except for the offerings of the musicians. But, of course, the ministry of music is always understood not to require ordination any more than it requires a professional fee for services rendered.

But what *is* restricted to the ministry of the properly authorized priesthood officers is officiating in the ordinances and sacraments of the church. No one else, under any circumstance, may replace the priesthood member in good standing when a person is to be baptized, confirmed, ordained, blessed, married, or to receive the Lord's Supper.

Differentiation in Priesthood

The list of officers previously mentioned suggests a variety of roles available to the church. It permits a high degree of specialization among the offices. These officers are organized for service in the following manner.[12]

There is a "standing ministry" that serves the local church, primarily comprising members of the Aaronic priesthood in the offices of deacon, teacher, and priest. These ministers are called to visit in the homes of the local members and to serve in the local church. The deacon has primary responsibility for church properties and the comforts of the congregation. The teacher has a teaching role that relates to a member's integration into the ongoing life of the congregation. It includes assisting in alleviating any factors that may prevent that integration. The priest officiates in the significant ordinances of baptism, sacrament of the Lord's Supper, marriage, and, in some instances, the ordination of other Aaronic priesthood members. The priest is also to "preach, teach, expound, exhort... and visit the house of each member..." (Doctrine and Covenants 17:10ab).

Another minister that may usually be thought of as being a "standing minister" is the elder. The office of elder is the primary office of the Melchisedec priesthood: all others in this priesthood, though they may have other duties specified by office title, are nevertheless elders. Those elders who serve in the local congregation are a part of the standing ministry. As spiritual leaders, the elders may officiate in sacraments requiring the laying on of hands: confirmation, blessing of children, administration to the sick, and ordination of other elders, priests, teachers and deacons. They may also serve in any of the functions of the Aaronic priesthood offices. Most pastors are elders, or members of the Melchisedec priesthood.

The members of the Quorums of Seventy are also elders who have been "set apart" through ordination to serve the unique function of evangelistic outreach. They are traveling ministers (as compared with standing ministers), and may be sent by an apostle on specific assignments of outreaching ministry. They are unusually gifted in witnessing and bringing converts into the church, which permits them to go into new fields and organize congregations of new members there.

High priests are elders who are qualified through spiritual gifts and maturity of experience so that they may be given demanding assignments of heavy responsibility. They usually serve in key administrative roles, such as stake presidents, district presidents, and regional administrators. They may also serve as members of high councils (such as stake high councils and the Standing High Council of the World Church). Although most high priests are standing ministers in that they serve in local church settings, many others are traveling ministers, often differentiated by being "set apart" through ordination to serve as apostles, evangelists, bishops, and members of the Quorum of the First Presidency.

Apostles are high priests who are members of the Council of Twelve. As a council, they share in establishing the church's missionary program and are responsible for the administration of the church throughout the world. Individual apostles usually have specific territories of the world for which they are responsible in administration and outreaching ministries.

Evangelists, sometimes also called patriarchs, are high priests who are freed from administrative responsibility so they can give attention solely to the spiritual life of the church. The president of their order is called the presiding evangelist. They, too, like the Twelve and the Seventy, have an evangelistic focus to their ministry—but especially a spiritual concern for the Saints as individuals. They are usually traveling ministers and may be called on to give a unique spiritual blessing to individuals who seek it, through the laying on of hands.

Bishops are high priests who are traveling ministers, too, although some may be normally assigned to local organizations of the church. The Presiding Bishopric of three bishops presides over the Order of Bishops; they are the chief financial officers of the church. They delegate much of their responsibility to bishops who serve the local churches throughout the world. Their focus on temporalities helps church members to integrate their stewardship of physical, financial, and temporal matters in the context of spiritual insight and eternal purposes.

The Quorum of the First Presidency includes three high priests, one of whom is the president of the church as well as "prophet, seer and revelator" to the church. The other two are counselors to the president and also carry the title of "president." All are called by an incumbent president through a revelatory document presented to and approved by a World Conference as representing the mind and will of God. Other officers called in this manner are apostles, members of the Presiding Bishopric, and the presiding evangelist.

Authority in Priesthood

Brother Xyz, a faithful priesthood member for many years, left the Reorganized Church of Jesus Christ of Latter Day Saints. He did not really want to, but after he was silenced for administrative reasons, it seemed to be the only face-saving thing for him to do. He had refused to accept the ordination of women, which not only placed him in opposition to church doctrine and practice, but it meant he no longer accepted the authority of church leaders and conference actions. He could no longer serve as an authorized representative of the organization. This alienated him from fellow ministers whom he accused of departing from the faith by accepting women into the priesthood. Hurt feelings abounded on both sides.

In view of the circumstances, in an attempt to stand for what he thought was right and at the same time save some remnant of what he considered to be his divine call to serve God in the priesthood, he voluntarily left the church for an association with others of similar opinion, where he was accepted on the basis of his original baptism and ordination in the RLDS Church.

What is the status of Brother Xyz's authority to represent the priesthood? to represent God? to represent the Reorganized Church of Jesus Christ of Latter Day Saints? to represent the new association of former RLDS members? In fact, what is authority when we are talking about priesthood?

Authority to represent someone is delegated. It is a power given by one party to another party, to represent or stand in the stead of the first party. Because it is delegated power, it is given as a privilege that may be withdrawn. The giver has that right.

In the case of priesthood in the RLDS Church, there are various kinds of authority in operation concurrently. In today's church, as far as what is practicable is concerned, probably no one kind of authority is sufficient to assure a vesting of authority. To serve and to provide an efficacious ministry, all of them are needed.

In practical terms, we recognize that there are at least four kinds of authority: spiritual or divine authority; legal authority; moral authority; and popular authority.

Popular authority is the authority of the people. By using this term, it is not necessarily implied that the minister enjoys the status of celebrity and popularity. Rather it means simply that some segment of the population recognizes the person as a legitimate minister. This authority is given by that population to someone whom they respect, admire, trust, and choose to be a leader who exercises authority over them. Without this authority, no one can really serve at all if the people they intend to serve do not accept them. In a certain area of American religious life, Billy Graham has popular authority. For a time, Jim Bakker did, too. In everyone's home town, there would be one or more ministers who possess popular authority. And in every RLDS congregation, most if not all priesthood members would be recognized as having this authority.

Within the scope of popular authority, there is a subcategory demanding more and more attention from the church. It is the authority of **competence**. The level of competence in its ministers with which the church feels comfortable is determined by the sentiments of the people. This manifestation of popular authority is an additional means by which people judge whether or not someone is capable of bearing the responsibility of ministry. It, too, is judged subjectively, but with the offering of advanced studies in the many fields touching on ministry, the symbol of an advanced degree suggests a level of competence in the particular areas studied. But there is no guarantee that the possessor of an advanced degree is a better minister than one without it.

Higher levels of competence in ministry have been demanded by church members in recent decades. This is largely due to two factors. They have seen the relationship between advanced studies and competence in their own professions and in the qualifications frequently required in those wishing to serve. There has been a carryover into their religious life and a respect for those who possess advanced degrees. Second, the influence on the population by television in general and televangelism in particular has caused church members to become accustomed to a professional quality of public speaking and musical performance. At church, these two factors tend to create an expectation of competence in public ministry and dissatisfaction when those expectations are not met.

Current expectations within the church vary to some degree from culture to culture. In the Western world, programs of study have been developed to assist a person in developing competence. At three different levels of preparation (high school, college, and postgraduate), the Temple School Center offers courses that have been very popular among Saints who wish to study. Many of these courses have been translated into several languages for use in various cultures, along with materials indigenous to those areas. It is now expected that all ordinands will have a certain level of preordination training and education, enabling their competence as they begin their ministry.

Full-time ministers in the church are usually salaried professionals, although some volunteers freely accept full-time roles without remuneration. A growing number of capable professional people, upon retirement, find a fulfilling second career in the ministry. Many of them serve without remuneration, while others are salaried.

The bulk of the ministry performed in the church, however, is done by part-time volunteers who freely give of themselves beyond the demands of their career employment. This is not likely to change. A major cornerstone of the Restoration movement is the universal calling to service. With that calling comes the opportunity to serve. Every member has, as a spiritual birthright, this calling to significant service as a minister. Not all will be ordained, but all will be given the opportunity to serve competently. Training and education are essential parts of the call.

All ministers, whether salaried or unsalaried, full-time or part-time, are under the same expectations of competence. With greater responsibility comes greater expectations. Appointee ministers, for example, are expected to complete a master's degree in religion shortly after accepting full-time ministry. Most of them would already have obtained an advanced degree in some other profession before entering full-time ministry.

Competence, and consequently education, have become virtual prerequisites to popular authority in the church in recent years.

Moral authority is given by the culture in which one is called to minister. Culture is a general process that is both shaper of, and is shaped by, the people. Morality is, therefore, always, to some degree, in flux—changing and changeable. Some of us who have lived long enough can testify to significant moral changes that have occurred in our own culture in our lifetime.

Those who possess moral authority can always be recognized because they stand for principles judged to be righteous by society. When their words are heard, not only by our ears but especially with our hearts, then we have recognized the moral authority with which they speak. And when their noble actions call forth an assenting nobility within us, our own righteousness is made more complete, and we become righteous people.

Culture tells us what is moral and gives morality its name. Because culture interacts with the people, and shapes them even as they shape it, it is represented by the people. Therefore moral authority can also be thought of as a kind of popular authority. Over many years of history of people and their culture, there develops a body of moral laws that are generally understood and enforced by civil law and custom and habit.

If a person is an outstanding example of the highest qualities vouchsafed in the mores of the culture, that person will be looked up to, revered, and emulated. Such a person possesses moral authority to represent the truth about morality as it is understood in that culture. If a person violates the moral laws of the culture, the authority to represent it is lost. It was because of a loss of moral authority that several televangelists lost their popular authority.

Legal authority is a formal kind of authority, granted by a person, organization, or association, delegating to another person the legal power to represent them before all other civil parties, individuals, organizations, institutions, governments, and all other entities. For whatever reason may seem good to the first party, legal authority may be withdrawn.

Most business transactions, virtually all judicial proceedings, and even the most menial of tasks require this delegation of legal authority. We would not permit a surgeon to operate, an officer to arrest a speeder, or a sanitary worker to service a septic tank if they were not legally authorized to do so. We want their activities to be done correctly, and we trust them because an authorizing agency, representing us and the whole society, has licensed them to do what they do. It may be possible that other people are equally capable to do these tasks. But we do not know that; therefore, we expect them to pass the examination and requirements of a licensing agency to whom we have delegated the authority to make that decision for us. If they expect us to accord them the privilege of serving us or acting on our behalf, they must be legally authorized.

In the field of religion, it is usually true that the authority to legally represent a church is granted by the church's licensing authority on whatever basis they deem necessary. Factors in consideration are training; education; and action by a conference, synod, district, convention, or other authorizing person(s) as required by their internal statutes. Ordination may also be required.

Spiritual authority, or divine authority, is difficult to define. Because it is always subjectively determined, one may claim divine authority from any experience that, to them, seems inspired of God. Others may differ entirely about the matter. There are no objective criteria everyone can use to decide the issue.

It is not unusual for some people to accept one person's claim to spiritual authority, while others may be adamantly in opposition—with both groups, all the while, claiming that God had inspired their positions! The only real claim to spiritual authority is that which functions pragmatically within a body of people who are agreed as to the criteria they will use in making their judgment. Often those criteria are undefined or poorly defined, but nevertheless generally agreed on and accepted by the body.

For example, following a particularly moving sermon, many people may agree that the speaker had authority to speak for God, but they may or may not be able to tell you why. Perhaps the message was timely and taken to heart. Perhaps the means of delivery employed by the speaker was emotionally moving and, thus, was equated by the majority with "spirituality." Perhaps one or more of the "gifts of the Spirit" were included in the content of the sermon. Perhaps the speaker testified with eloquence about ministries that had been accompanied by the Holy Spirit's intervention, and the very telling of the stories became inspirational to the hearers.

For these and many other personal reasons, people may believe that a given person possesses divine authority to represent God. The criteria used to make this judgment are generally accepted and understood by the group, but they are always subjective and tend to operate informally within the group.

It can be argued by some—and probably successfully—that God can give and withdraw divine authority according to God's own criteria and purposes. Our difficulty in knowing what God does in granting or retracting this authority is the difficulty we have in knowing the mind and will of God. No one person, or even all members of the body together, possess enough information and spiritual insight to be able to say that we know, in all instances, what God's purposes and intentions are. Frequently, we even have difficulty in recognizing what God has done before our very eyes! As a result, we have little to rely on in determining when a person has or does not have divine authority.

We usually rely on other forms of authority to indicate when divine authority is lost. And some would assume that if the other forms have been lost for good cause, it is an indication that the divine authority was either lost previously or concurrently.

Scripturally, some would say that the right to exercise this sort of divine authority has been granted to the church by Christ, when he said, "...and whatsoever thou shalt bind on earth, shall be bound in heaven; and whatsoever thou shalt loose on earth, shall be loosed in heaven" (Matthew 16:20). They would maintain that the church, therefore, has the privilege and power to decide questions of divine authority. However, this authority to "bind on earth" is in fact a form of legal authority and functions as such.

To return to Brother Xyz: What authority did he take with him when he left the RLDS Church and began a new relationship with another group? He no longer held legal authority from the RLDS Church as a minister, because he had been silenced. To whatever degree he still was a moral man, he may have held some moral authority. If, however, he behaved in unethical ways in making the transition, his moral authority could be in question. Popular authority is in the eyes of the beholder: If some people still respected him as "their" minister, then they would be willing to receive him as their minister. Many others would withdraw such authority from him. As far as the spiritual authority is concerned, that is, the sense of divine calling which he felt he had received from God and that no one could take away from him, he might still believe he had such authority. But it will do him no good until he finds a group of people who accept his testimony about that, for divine authority is a subjective matter.

To illustrate the difficulty of the question and the dilemma that it presents, look at a particular situation. Suppose a couple comes to him and asks him to marry them. He proceeds to honor their request. Remember, he was accepted by his new associates on the basis of his original baptism and ordination. Does he have moral authority to marry? Perhaps, depending on his own personal moral character, and whether or not he advocates moral and ethical behavior. Does he have popular authority to perform the ceremony? Perhaps, if the people composing the religious association and the bride's and groom's families accord him that authority.

In a marriage, there are two areas of legal authority to be considered. As far as the authority to represent the RLDS Church is concerned, that legal authority was withdrawn. If the new association formally agreed among themselves to grant him authority to function in sacraments and ordinances, then he has their legal authority. But that is not the end of the issue; we must also ask if he has *civil* authority to perform marriages. A wedding that is sanctioned by law carries civil as well as religious implications. Unless the new association has created a new legal entity and has provided some authorizing procedure acceptable to the civil authorities, he may not be qualified to represent civil government in performing marriages. The couples he marries may not be legally married at all as far as civil law is concerned.

Does he have divine authority to administer the sacrament of marriage? On a practical, human level, this would fall into the same category as popular authority. It would be granted or withheld by the individuals who believe that he possesses divine authority and who are willing to regard him as a divinely-called minister. But on an ultimate level, only God can give or take away truly divine authority, and we have no objective way of measuring that. If God chooses to place the responsibility for such a matter in the hands of God's own chosen servants, then we have the authority of a theocracy operating to determine the boundaries of divine authority. This issue then becomes more a matter of legal authority as determined by the authorities of a given church, God's chosen representatives.

Is it possible for God to act in ways that appear to be outside the usual, ordinary policies described in scripture and traditionalized by practice? When questions of authority are involved, is God bound to follow the same guidelines at all times and in all circumstances? Can we ever establish the final criteria for a properly executed divine call and assume that God will always act within those time-honored and revealed criteria? Or is God free to do whatever God wants to do?

Obviously, if we believe God is omnipotent, or even if we only believe that God is a free agent, then we must grant that God can do whatever God wants to do in regard to whom God chooses as divinely authorized priesthood. The scriptures and church history provide ample testimony of this being the case. When Joseph Smith and Oliver Cowdery received Aaronic priesthood authority—and later the Melchisedec authority—the procedures that we are now accustomed to expect were not in place. It required extraordinary acts on the part of an angelic messenger in conferring the Aaronic priesthood, and on the part of the nascent church in the case of the Melchisedec priesthood, for this transfer of representative power to occur. There were no precedents; there were no authorized conference bodies; there was no set of priesthood ministers to provide for the ordination. It required someone who had no parallel or equivalent authority to lay hands on the head of the ordinand, conferring a power that the first did not himself hold. This historic event, establishing the basis for authority in the Reorganized Church of Jesus Christ of Latter Day Saints, is, nevertheless, recognized as being fully and divinely sanctioned. God is considered to be quite able to do whatever God wants to do in delegating divine authority.

The Book of Mormon tells the story of another extraordinary event conveying authority to the spiritual leader Alma. Alma is described as a person, perhaps a priest, who had rebelled against God. He repents and begins, in a secluded area where he lives, to teach people some of the doctrines he had learned from the prophet Abinadi. This rather clandestine teaching results in many people wanting to participate with him in his religious activities. On a given day, and recognizing a lack of authority, the passage gives Alma's words, as he stands in water with his first candidate for baptism: "O Lord, pour out thy Spirit upon thy servant that he may do this work with holiness of heart" (Mosiah 9:43). It is a request for authority to proceed. Afterward, he baptizes Helam with a baptismal prayer more extemporaneous than ritualistic. Then both Alma and Helam are immersed—for neither had yet been baptized, and neither apparently possessed priesthood authority. After this time, the story tells that Alma ordained other priests, "having authority from God" (Mosiah 9:51).

The historical account of Joseph and Oliver, and the scriptural story of Alma and Helam, both suggest that divine authority to represent God may not easily be defined. It certainly cannot be confined "to our poor reach of mind," to borrow a phrase from George Rawson's hymn, "We Limit Not the Truth of God."

God is always capable of surprising us, just when we think that we have finished our study of God's methods and measures. There is always more to be learned on any subject when God is a part of the picture, and we do well to remain quite humble about how much we know, or think we know. The God who speaks from a burning bush, or through an angelic messenger, or out of the mouth of an itinerant rabbi bound for crucifixion, or with a blinding light on the road to Damascus is still capable of surprising us by means of light, fire, angel, or execution. But one thing is clearly understood by all, in every dispensation of time: It is God's intention to touch our lives with the Holy Spirit and to call us to divine service.

Conclusion

In resumé, we observe these things about the history of God's action toward humans through priesthood:

God takes the initiative in reaching toward humanity through the spirit of revelation. Humans then, naturally and easily, react to God's initiative. A part of that reaction is to feel favored and to experience a sense of a divine call.

Because of what is understood to be God's own initiative in making such a call, various elaborations of priestly function began to develop early in Hebrew history. The earliest functions were to consult the oracle (a prophetic function) in addition to the primary function of maintaining the faith and traditions of the people chosen by God. The function to officiate in sacrificial offerings became identified with priesthood after having originally been a nonpriesthood responsibility. A particular segment of the population, one of the Hebrew tribes, was identified for priesthood call and to officiate in these offices.

Ritual became more important after the priesthood became primarily responsible for sacrificial offering. Ritual purity was rigorously required. Priesthood practices evolved culturally, proliferating priesthood's functions and differentiating them with distinguishing characteristics. This occurred in measure with the increasing priesthood population and the complexity of the social order. The cultural context is clearly intertwined with changing priesthood roles, functions, and offices in the history of Old Testament Judaism.

The New Testament offers a continuation of the principle of cultural effect on priesthood. Christianity emerged within a Jewish culture, under Roman domination, in a patriarchal society. The impact of the new revelation in Jesus Christ and the relatedness of his ministry—and thus the church's—with culture resulted in a new approach to ministry. All were called to serve and to minister. The office of member, while not referred to as such, is clearly seen in the New Testament scriptures.

In time, as the church grew in size and geographic location, it found itself confronting many culturally determined issues. The need for multifaceted ministry in differing environments led to differentiation and proliferation of ministerial roles. New offices and new functions emerged.

In a corollary way, the traditional Jewish church hierarchy was deemphasized and virtually ignored by the New Testament church. The roles in the New Testament church structures were named and functionally described by their name in the stream of culture. As had been observed in early Hebrew tradition, access to priesthood was no longer limited to a chosen family, tribe, or nation, and priesthood was not confined to those who were qualified by a rigorous process of ritual purification. Nor was the opportunity to serve limited by cultural factors of race, sex, age, national origin, or slavery.

Inasmuch as priesthood roles were originally only identified by function and not clearly delineated as offices in the New Testament church, we are left with a linguistic puzzle to know if the female prophets and elders were also functionally employed (and ordained) in a ministerial context as were their ordained male counterparts.

The postapostolic church evolved with institutional development similar to that which evolved in Judaism: from a general, open call and responsibility placed on all, to a restricted, self-regulated, authoritarian clergy. In Christianity as in Judaism, institutional religion found itself in dialogue with God and with culture.

In the Restoration movement, scriptures that at first may be thought to suggest a universalistic view of priesthood on closer scrutiny appear to support nominalism and particularity. This is true on a philosophical basis in light of the views of Joseph Smith Jr. on the continuity and conservation of matter and life beyond the grave. It is also observed in Joseph Smith III's application of nominalistic views—a particular minister or class of ministers in a particular setting—in regard to the calling of blacks to priesthood responsibility. He reaffirmed in modern times that "all are called," and that their God-given gifts are to be respected in the scope of their ministry.

We learn from a review of our history that a nominalistic approach supports the call of women to priesthood. It also suggests that the many cultural differences present in the various world missions of the modern church call for an application of priesthood's functions and procedures in keeping with cultural diversity. That is, to achieve cultural equivalents on basic principles of priesthood in a new environment may require new approaches and not a simple copying of Western practices. What is elsewhere appropriate may be inappropriate in some nations. And priesthood appears to be so particular in its application that some may be called to function according to gifts appropriate only to their own cultural context.

From the many things we have discussed in this book, we may deduce several implications for priesthood and its function within an international church. For one thing, it suggests that the church is collectively responsible for its stewardship over the priesthood and members it has called. These ministers are gifts of God to the church, and the church must not leave them alone to fend for themselves without leadership, resources, and an opportunity to fulfill their calling. As they bring their gifts to the altar of service, they should be accepted with thanksgiving and utilized to the highest degree possible. Because of their calling, they have a mandate to offer ministry and service in the name of God.

Second, the individual member and priesthood ordinand also have a responsibility and stewardship to fulfill and, hopefully in some degree at least, to magnify. To magnify one's calling does not suggest simply a replication of the habits and customs of ministry offered by others whom we have observed. It instead holds forth the option of so serving that the future definition of what it means to be a deacon or elder or apostle or member will be altered, at least in the minds of some, because of the enlarged scope and depth of ministry offered by this newly ordained minister, or newly baptized member.

Third, for those called to priestly roles and functions, it also suggests that an accountability is appropriate for both their use and disuse of the gifts of God to them. The means of accountability may necessarily vary from time to time. But it is a blessing to the individual and to the church for priesthood members to follow the disciplines of self-accounting, and to have the opportunity to discuss one's self-accounting with another minister. This same accountability should well be engaged for every member of the body but must begin with those who have accepted the additional responsibility of priesthood calling.

The story of priesthood that has unfolded in these pages is a dramatic, surprising, captivating, and inviting account. For many of us, it is our story—we readily identify with priests and prophets throughout the ages. Somehow, they are our kin, our ancestors, and we are their descendants, of their lineage.

It is a story that is a dialogue between humankind and God, an ongoing conversation that is not finished, nor can it be as long as this world needs continuing guidance from on high. But at its ultimate reach, it is a story that is so close to each of us that we can say, "It is mine. Priesthood exists for my sake—as my minister, as my spiritual counselor and guide." And in the same caught breath, with an emotion that stirs us to our innermost self, we also must say, "It is mine, too, as a servant called of God, to be a minister for others' sake."

Notes

1. *Hymns of the Saints* (Independence, Missouri: Herald House, 1981). No. 213, "I Sought the Lord"; Anonymous, 1880; revised in *The Pilgrim Hymnal*, 1904.
2. William G. Dever, *Recent Archeological Discoveries and Biblical Research* (Seattle, Washington: University of Washington Press, 1990), 164.
3. *Times and Seasons* 3 (August 1, 1842): 865–866.
4. *Messenger and Advocate* 1 (October 1834): 15–16.
5. S. R. Driver, *An Introduction to the Literature of the Old Testament* (New York: Merriam Books, 1960), 154–155.
6. Herbert G. May, "Introduction" to the Book of Ezekiel, *The Interpreter's Bible*, Volume VI (New York: Abingdon Press, 1956), 44–45.
7. *A Select Library of the Nicene and Post-Nicene Fathers of the Christian Church*, Volume XI, Saint Chrysostom; edited by Philip Schaff (Grand Rapids, Michigan: William B. Eerdmans Publishing, 1978), 555.
8. *Études Bibliques, Saint Paul, Épître Aux Romains*, M.-J. Lagrange, M.-J. Lagrange; P. Fages (Paris, 1915); Librairie Lecoffre, J. Gabalda et Compagnie, éditeurs (Paris, 1950), 366.
9. C. E. B. Cranfield, *A Critical and Exegetical Commentary on the Epistle to the Romans*, vol. II (Edinburgh: T. & T. Clark, 1975), 788–789.
10. Bernadette J. Brooten, *Women Leaders in the Ancient Synagogue, Inscriptional Evidence and Background Issues* (Chico, California: Scholars Press, 1982), 1.
11. Ibid., 22.
12. For a more complete discussion of this subject, see *The Priesthood Manual* (Independence, Missouri: Herald House, 1990).

Bibliography and Suggested Readings

Anderson, Bernard W. *Understanding the Old Testament.* Englewood Cliffs, New Jersey: Prentice-Hall, 1966.

Bergmann, Gustav. *Meaning and Existence.* Madison, Wisconsin: University of Wisconsin Press, 1960.

Bewer, Julius A. *The Literature of the Old Testament.* New York: Columbia University Press, 1933.

Brooten, Bernadette J. *Women Leaders in the Ancient Synagogue.* Chico, California: Scholars Press, 1982.

Coriden, James. *Sexism and Church Law.* New York: Paulist Press, 1977.

Daniel-Rops, Henri. *Daily Life in the Time of Jesus.* Translated by Patrick O'Brian. New York: Hawthorne Books, 1963.

Dempsey, Elbert A., Jr. *The Power of the Prophetic.* Independence, Missouri: Herald House, 1988.

_____. *Untangling Our Faith.* Independence, Missouri: Herald House, 1993.

Dever, William G. *Recent Archaeological Discoveries and Biblical Research.* Seattle, Washington: University of Washington Press, 1990.

Dictionary of the Bible. Edited by James Hastings, D.D. New York York: Charles Scribner's Sons, 1937.

Driver, S. R. *An Introduction to the Literature of the Old Testament.* New York: Merriam Books, 1960.

Edersheim, Alfred, M.A., D.D., Ph.D. *The Temple.* London: James Clarke and Company, 1959.

Flanders, Henry Jackson, Jr., Robert Wilson Crapps, and David Anthony Smith. *People of the Covenant: An Introduction to the Old Testament.* New York: The Ronald Press, 1963.

Foakes-Jackson, F. J. *A Brief Biblical History.* New York: Richard R. Smith, 1930.

Gardiner, Anne Marie. *Women in Catholic Priesthood: An Expanded Vision.* Mahwah, New Jersey: Paulist Press, 1976.

Gilkey, Langdon. *Naming the Whirlwind: The Renewal of God-Language.* New York: Bobbs Merrill, 1969.

Hospers, John. *Readings in Aesthetics*. New York: The Free Press, 1969.
Howard, J. Grant. *The Trauma of Transparency: A Biblical Approach to Interpersonal Communication*. Sisters, Oregon: Multnomah Press, 1982.
Jewett, Paul K. *The Ordination of Women*. Grand Rapids, Michigan: William B. Eerdmans Publishing, 1982.
Jewish Encyclopedia. Vol. X. New York: Funk and Wagnalls, 1912.
McFague, Sallie. *Metaphorical Theology*. Philadelphia: Fortress Press, 1982.
Oberman, Helco. *The Harvest of Medieval Theology (Nominalism)*. Grand Rapids, Michigan: William B. Eerdmans Publishing, 1962.
Maitland, Sara. *A Map of the New Country Women and Christianity*. New York: Routledge and Kegan Paul, 1983.
Pfeiffer, Robert H. *Introduction to the Old Testament*. New York: Harper and Brothers, 1948.
Plantinga, Alvin. *The Nature of Necessity*. New York: Oxford Press, 1974.
Priesthood Manual, The. (Independence, Missouri: Herald House, 1990).
Prymak, Gregory. *Authority in the RLDS Theological Tradition: Two Views*, Theological Monograph Series. Independence, Missouri: Graceland/Park Press, 1995.
Richardson, Alan, and John Bowden. *The Westminster Dictionary of Christian Theology*. Philadelphia: Westminster Press, 1983.
Sandmel, Samuel. *The Hebrew Scriptures: An Introduction to Their Literature and Religious Ideas*. New York: Oxford University Press, 1978.
Smith, J. B. *Greek-English Concordance to the New Testament*. Scottdale, Pennsylvania: Herald Press, 1955.
Smith-Kemp. *The Credibility of Divine Existence*. London: McMillan, 1967.
Snyder, Henry. *The Persistence of Spiritual Ideals in English Letters*. Nashville, Tennessee: Cokesbury Press, 1922.
Warkentin, Marjorie. *Ordination: A Biblical-Historical View*. Grand Rapids, Michigan: William B. Eerdmans Publishing, 1982.

Study Guide

The following questions and activities will aid facilitators in using *Priesthood: For Others' Sake* in classroom settings. For convenience they are organized according to the seven sections of the book. However, because those sections are of unequal length, facilitators will need to adapt them depending on the number of class sessions scheduled and the particular emphasis desired. Class participants may find it helpful to read the entire text once before beginning their detailed study of the book.

I. From Revelation to Priestly Society
1. Share situations when you have been surprised by God and when you have deliberately sought divine assistance.
2. The idea of a called and chosen people was promoted by Israelite prophets up until the late settlement of Canaan and the establishment of the monarchy, then resumed during the Babylonian exile. Why would "divine chosenness" be more appropriate for Israelites during their weak and vulnerable times than during prosperous eras? What can we learn about being called and chosen by God as a result?
3. What is the difference between being chosen by God to *do* and to *be*?
4. To what extent are we Christians justified in using Hebrew/Judaic images in regard to minis-

try? Is this more of an evolutionary or revolutionary process?

5. Define the ancient concept of theocratic government. When did democratic elements begin to appear?
6. Compare the functioning of Israel's priests, who supported and maintained the status quo, and prophets, who for the most part revealed new understandings. How well did these two roles complement one another, or were they almost always at odds?
7. What was the importance of Ezra's reforms for Israel's religious life, especially in regard to a return to orthodox belief at the sacrifice of compassion? How did the sheer numbers of priests influence Israel's development?
8. With the establishment of a strong monarchy and central government under David and Solomon, in what ways did priesthood's role become an "arm of the king"? How did this affect Israel's religious practices?

II. Two Theologies of Priesthood

9. Compare the testimonies of Joseph Smith Jr. and Oliver Cowdery related to their spiritual experience with an angel identified as John the Baptist. Include common elements, differences, and basic approaches. How does your perception of this event change by seeing it as either a literal happening or a "spiritual vision"? Is there a clear understanding as to which it was? What is the importance of an angelic messenger here?
10. What purpose for priesthood can be inferred from these testimonies?

11. How did this and other incidents tend to differentiate and isolate Latter Day Saints from more traditional, mainstream Christian groups?
12. What happens with questions of authority, validity, and consequences when you deal with seemingly competing and contradictory visions?
13. How can we avoid associating the holiness of the revelatory process of prophecy with either the prophet or the person designated by the prophet? What are some of the consequences?
14. What does it mean for priesthood to be described with the following terms: preexistent, eternal, absolute, universal?
15. Is it possible for priesthood to be *both* "particular" and "universal"? Why or why not? Is this the same as asking if priesthood is limited to current circumstances or of an eternal nature?
16. In considering whether an individual's priesthood goes beyond mortal life, what areas of concern are raised? Has this been, or is it now, an accepted doctrine, tradition, or teaching of the RLDS Church? How have RLDS teachings differed from LDS (Mormon) beliefs?
17. How does Joseph Smith Jr.'s statement recorded in Doctrine and Covenants 90:5 that "the elements are eternal" relate to the idea of the universality of priesthood? Compare the thoughts of Thomas Aquinas and the scientific principle of conservation of matter (see pages 27–28).
18. The author identifies three compelling reasons why it is difficult to accept priesthood universally or absolutely, independent from any particular expression (see page 29). Briefly outline each reason and discuss the implications. Do you

agree or disagree with his assertion that a "nominalistic view of priesthood as existing in the particular individuals who are called to be priests may be indicated"?
19. How does this issue relate to the idea of One True Church governed by a priesthood hierarchy that stands in the stead of Jesus Christ?

III. The Unfolding Panorama of Priesthood

20. Joseph Smith Jr.'s scriptural emendations (recorded in the Doctrine and Covenants and the Inspired Version of the Bible) add priesthood responsibilities for ancient figures such as Adam, Seth, Enoch, and Noah. If taken literally, what effect do these emendations have on one's understandings of priesthood's functioning, especially in regard to sacrificial offerings?
21. What did the Levites do in Israelite religious life? How did their role change over time?
22. Describe the function of the ancient Urim and Thummim (see pages 32–33). What were the limits of this prophetic oracle?
23. What role did lineage play in the Levitical priesthood, and how was this related to use of the Urim and Thummim?
24. List the four major priestly functions during the time of the monarchy (see page 36). Does this in any way help us today in understanding priesthood ministry? If so, how?
25. Because the monarchy strongly promoted the Jerusalem Temple as the "proper place" for rituals over tribal sanctuaries in Shiloh and Bethel, in particular, Israelite religion became highly centralized. What were some of the pros and cons

of this? Can it be helpful for us in considering centralization or decentralization in our religious practices?
26. The author ties the tremendous growth in numbers of Israelite priests to an increased need for specialization and qualifying training/education. How common is such a trend among religious groups, including our own? What are some of the consequences?

IV. Two Models for Priestly Ministry
27. How well could Jesus have attacked the corrupt religious institutions of his day if he had not been so steeped in Jewish heritage?
28. In what ways was Jesus' message of "good news" a departure from traditional Jewish faith? In what ways was it a transformation or continuation?
29. Compare the following positions:
    • traditional Hebrew understanding that priests were professions of a particular lineage chosen as intermediaries between God and humankind;
    • basic Christian understanding that all are called to serve one another within a "royal priesthood" of all believers.
30. In what ways did the emerging Christian fellowship break with the hierarchies of both Hebrew patriarchal society and Roman social organization? How long did it take before Christian communities began to develop male-dominated hierarchies? Why?
31. Define "theocracy." How did it function in ancient Palestine under Roman occupation?

32. Eventually the Christian Church split into western (Roman Catholic) and eastern (Orthodox) branches. Describe the hierarchical models of priesthood in each. How were they tied to authoritarian theologies and practices? Why would the author include the LDS (Mormon) model with them?
33. In what ways did the Protestant Reformation confront the existing traditions of Catholicism? Where did the reformers get their models for priesthood and what kind of changes took place?

Ordinations and Offices
34. What's the difference between a disciple and an apostle?
35. Discuss the calling of "the seventy" as described in Luke 10. Who were they, what were they supposed to do, and how did their presence affect the infant Christian community?
36. What ministerial functions were needed most in the early years of the Christian Church? Which familiar functions today were not introduced until later? Why?
37. Read Acts 2:42–47. What does this passage tell us about the believers' community?
38. How did the role of Jewish synagogue functionaries (see page 49 ff.) translate into Christian communities?
39. What was the function and/or office of the seven individuals referred to in Acts 6:1–7? Discuss the procedure of "ordaining" them.
40. Which came first: bishops, deacons, elders, priests, or evangelists? Why is it difficult to ascertain for sure?

41. What's the difference between "lukewarm members" and those who serve faithfully in the "office of member"?
42. On a chalkboard or large sheets of newsprint, list the following English-language words and their Greek counterparts: deacon, teacher, priest, elder/presbyter, bishop, apostle, evangelist, prophet. What was the original meaning of each?
43. Compare the two meanings for prophet: one who "foretells" or "tells forth."

Women Disciples
44. In the story of Mary and Martha with Jesus (see Luke 10:38–42) who is this really about? What was the attitude behind each woman's actions?
45. What important roles did women play in the early church? How did they reflect and/or contradict the customs, traditions, and rules of Jews and Gentiles?
46. How did caring for widows enter significantly in Apostle Paul's letters?
47. Who were Phoebe, Priscilla, Jael, and Junia? Why is each woman's experience and example important?
48. Some modern translations of Romans 16:7 alter the spelling of Junia's name to its masculine equivalent, although that name is found nowhere else in any writings of the time period. What would cause translators to do that?
49. What are the advantages and dangers in supporting our current RLDS practice of ordaining women solely on the basis of interpretations of these biblical passages?

Wolves among the Flock
50. Who were the "grievous wolves" referred to in Acts 20:29? Why was Paul so concerned with them? What does this incident tell us about the early church and its struggles over leadership?
51. How and why did a priestly class come to stand between the body of Christian believers and God? How did the symbols and images of the clergy reinforce the earlier male domination already prevalent in Judaism?
52. What changes took place in Christianity when the Roman Empire began to conquer the world "with the sign of the cross"?
53. Compare Galatians 3:28 to the rigid divisions that had grown within the church of "priesthood and members, clergy and laity, leaders and followers, the powerful and the powerless." Could the church have developed in different directions? What circumstances and influences would have had to be different?

V. Priesthood in the Reorganization
54. How was the issue of ordaining black men dealt with in the early years of the Reorganization? What societal factors outside the church were involved? What lasting effects on race relations and ordination policy have resulted?
55. In what ways does the particular example of ordaining blacks in the late 1800s inform the more universal understanding and practices of ordination in the RLDS Church?
56. Read Doctrine and Covenants 119:8b. What does it say in regard to the roles of member and priesthood?

57. The author states that "while the office of member is universal, the office of priesthood is not to be applied universally." What does this statement mean, and what are some of the contingent factors related to this topic?

VI. Priesthood Today

58. On a chalkboard or large sheets of newsprint, list the following topics: Hebrew/Jewish priesthood; New Testament church; Middle Ages; Renaissance; Protestant Reformation; Restoration movement founders; early Reorganization. List our "inheritances" from each source and discuss the positive and negative aspects of each. Why do some items show up on more than one list?
59. Why was the concept of lineage so important in ancient Judaism? How did this influence the early Restoration movement as well as the early years of the Reorganization? How much has the idea of lineage diminished in the modern RLDS Church? Why?
60. Briefly outline the necessary steps for ordination. What are the supporting reasons for each?
61. What are some of the expectations placed on ordinands and the RLDS community in regard to the person ordained?
62. Do you agree with the statement that every ablebodied man or woman in the church has a potential calling to priesthood? Discuss your reasons for or against.
63. List in two columns the typical congregational duties which either do or do not require ordination. Would you move any functions from one list

to the other? Which functions? Why? If so, how would you achieve this change?

64. What are the theological reasons behind requiring priesthood to officiate in the sacraments? How can nonordained people "assist" them?

Differentiation in Priesthood

65. Which priesthood offices usually compose the "standing ministry"? Describe their duties and functions.
66. Which priesthood offices may be considered "traveling ministry"? Describe their duties and functions.
67. Which priesthood offices are actually categories within the larger designation of "high priests"? What function do they serve in local settings and in the World Church? Where did the RLDS office of high priest originate?
68. Which World Church officers are now called by the prophet-president of the church? How has the calling procedure changed in the Reorganization (see the introductory comments to Doctrine and Covenants Section 117 and the following: Section 132:1–2, 135:1, 136:1, 138:1–2, and 148:5–8)?

Authority in Priesthood

69. Using the example of Brother Xyz (see page 84 ff.), discuss the following terms: popular authority, authority of competence, moral authority, legal authority, and spiritual authority. It may be helpful to list them on separate sheets of newsprint or a chalkboard along with concise definitions.

70. What areas of authority should be considered in regard to officiating at a wedding? What is the relationship between civil and religious obligations? What are some of the implications that arise?
71. Is it possible for God to act in ways that appear to be outside the usual, ordinary policies described in scripture and traditionalized by practice? Must God follow the same guidelines in all circumstances? How can we be certain it is God's Spirit and not humans who do the initiating?
72. Compare the examples of Joseph Smith Jr. and Oliver Cowdery (see page 94) and Book of Mormon characters Alma and Helam (see page 95). Why is it hard to define divine authority?
73. Read the words of George Rawson's familiar hymn, "We Limit Not the Truth of God" (*Hymns of the Saints*, No. 309). In what ways does this hymn speak to the issue of priesthood authority? Why has the hymn become such an enduring favorite among RLDS people?

VII. Conclusion

74. What are some of the implications we can deduce for priesthood and its function within an international church (see pages 100–101)?
75. How can the centuries-old story of priesthood within Judaism, Christianity, and the Restoration movement become "our story" today? What parts of the story do we emphasize or reject?
76. What has been most helpful to you in using this book on priesthood? most disturbing? What unanswered questions have arisen?

About the Author

Alan D. Tyree served as a full-time appointee minister for the Reorganized Church of Jesus Christ of Latter Day Saints (RLDS) for more than forty-one years and was honorably retired as a member of the Quorum of the First Presidency after serving as a counselor for ten years. Before that President Tyree served for sixteen years as a member of the Quorum of Twelve Apostles.

A Phi Beta Kappa graduate of the University of Iowa, with a degree in music and minors in education and religion, he later took postgraduate studies in French and anthropology at the Columbia and Kansas City campuses of the University of Missouri.

He is well known as a writer, editor, translator, hymn writer, and as a frequent performer on the bassoon and saxophone (occasionally also clarinet, flute, or oboe). He edited the revised edition of *Exploring the Faith* (Herald House, 1987) and authored the following Herald House books: *The Gospel Graced by a People* (1993) and *Evan Fry: Proclaimer of Good News* (Makers of Church Thought Series, 1995). He and his wife, Gladys, live in Independence, Missouri.